TRUE TO LIFE

ELEMENTARY

Joanne Collie
Stephen Slater

PERSONAL STUDY
WORKBOOK

CAMBRIDGE
UNIVERSITY PRESS

PUBLISHED BY THE PRESS SYNDICATE OF THE UNIVERSITY OF CAMBRIDGE
The Pitt Building, Trumpington Street, Cambridge, United Kingdom

CAMBRIDGE UNIVERSITY PRESS
The Edinburgh Building, Cambridge CB2 2RU, UK
40 West 20th Street, New York, NY 10011–4211, USA
477 Williamstown Road, Port Melbourne, VIC 3207, Australia
Ruiz de Alarcón 13, 28014 Madrid, Spain
Dock House, The Waterfront, Cape Town 8001, South Africa

http://www.cambridge.org

First published 1995
Seventh printing 2002

Printed in the United Kingdom at the University Press, Cambridge

ISBN 0 521 42140 3 Elementary Class Book
ISBN 0 521 42141 1 Elementary Personal Study Workbook
ISBN 0 521 42142 X Elementary Teacher's Book
ISBN 0 521 42143 8 Elementary Class Cassette Set
ISBN 0 521 42144 6 Elementary Personal Study Cassette
ISBN 0 521 48574 6 Elementary Personal Study Audio CD

CONTENTS

STARTER UNIT

What do you know? What can you remember?

Here are some exercises to help you learn – or remember – a few basic things about English.

1 How do you spell that?

the alphabet

A ▭ Do you know the English alphabet? Try to say the letters. Then listen and repeat, if you like.

A   B   C   D   E   F   G   H   I   J   K   L   M
N   O   P   Q   R   S   T   U   V   W   X   Y   Z

B ▭ Spell these words out loud. Then listen and repeat, if you like.

ARTURO   YAPRAK   HELGA   KENJI   ZORAN   BEN   WILLIAM
FRANCES   QUEEN   ENGLAND   MEXICO   VANCOUVER

2 One's the sun, two's the shoe

numbers

A Match the numbers with the rhyming picture. Number 1 is done for you.

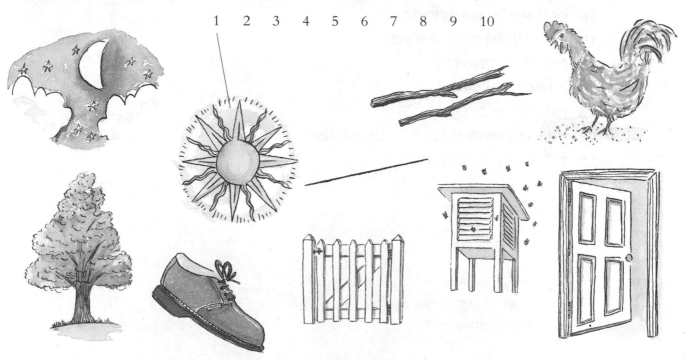

1   2   3   4   5   6   7   8   9   10

B ▭ Say these numbers. Then listen and repeat, if you like.

1   2   3   4   5   6   7   8   9   10   11   12   13   14
15   16   17   18   19   20   30   40   50   60   70   80   90   100

C ▭ Listen. When there is a pause, say the next number.

Example: *one two three* (pause) – you say *four*.

3 What time is it?

A Write the time. Then listen and check your answers.

1 morning 1. It's *seven o'clock* .... 2. It's ....

2 afternoon 3. It's .... 4. It's ....

3 evening 5. It's .... 6. It's ....

B Write the time. Then listen and check your answers.

1. It's .... 2. It's ....

C Look at the example.

Example:

It's three o'clock
in the morning.   *It's three o'clock*
in the afternoon.   *It's ten o'clock*
in the morning.   *It's ten o'clock*
in the evening.

 Write the time. Then listen and check your answers.

1. It's .... in the .... 3. It's .... in the ....

2. It's .... in the .... 4. It's .... in the ....

4 International times

A Look at this example.

The flight to Bucharest is at 8.45.
That's a quarter to nine in the morning.

RO871 Bucharest	08.45
AA007 New York	09.15
BA671 Delhi	10.35
AC081 Vancouver Toronto	11.20
THY 34 Istanbul	14. 20
LH667 Berlin	16.25
JAL223 Tokyo	18.15
SA67 Karachi	19.40

Complete the sentences.

1. The flight to New York is at 9.15. That's ....

2. The flight to Delhi is at 10.35. That's ....

3. The flight to Vancouver and Toronto is at 11.20. That's ....

4. The flight to Istanbul is at 14.20. That's ....

5. The flight to Berlin is at 16.25. That's ....

B Listen and put the time on the clocks. Number 1 is an example.

1. Bangkok   2. Sydney   3. Delhi   4. Cairo

C AM

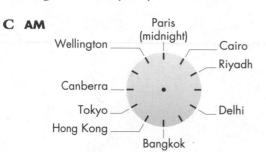

Wellington — Paris (midnight) — Cairo
Riyadh
Canberra
Tokyo — Delhi
Hong Kong
Bangkok

PM

London — (noon)
Vancouver
Brasilia
Caracas — Mexico City
New York

It's midnight in Paris. What time is it in …

1. New York?   It's …………………………… .
2. Bangkok?   It's …………………………… .
3. Tokyo?   It's …………………………… .
4. Vancouver?   It's …………………………… .
5. London?   It's …………………………… .
6. Riyadh?   It's …………………………… .
7. Wellington?   It's …………………………… .
8. Caracas?   It's …………………………… .
9. Cairo?   It's …………………………… .
10. Delhi?   It's …………………………… .

---

5 What day is it today?

days of the week, months of the year

YEAR PLANNER					

JANUARY

S	M	Tu	W	Th	F	S
						1
2	3	4	5	6	7	8
9	10	11	12	13	14	15
16	17	18	19	20	21	22
23/30	24/31	25	26	27	28	29

FEBRUARY

S	M	Tu	W	Th	F	S
		1	2	3	4	5
6	7	8	9	10	11	12
13	14	15	16	17	18	19
20	21	22	23	24	25	26
27	28					

MARCH

S	M	Tu	W	Th	F	S
		1	2	3	4	5
6	7	8	9	10	11	12
13	14	15	16	17	18	19
20	21	22	23	24	25	26
27	28	29	30	31		

APRIL

S	M	Tu	W	Th	F	S
					1	2
3	4	5	6	7	8	9
10	11	12	13	14	15	16
17	18	19	20	21	22	23
24	25	26	27	28	29	30

MAY

S	M	Tu	W	Th	F	S
1	2	3	4	5	6	7
8	9	10	11	12	13	14
15	16	17	18	19	20	21
22	23	24	25	26	27	28
29	30	31				

JUNE

S	M	Tu	W	Th	F	S
			1	2	3	4
5	6	7	8	9	10	11
12	13	14	15	16	17	18
19	20	21	22	23	24	25
26	27	28	29	30	31	

JULY

S	M	Tu	W	Th	F	S
					1	2
3	4	5	6	7	8	9
10	11	12	13	14	15	16
17	18	19	20	21	22	23
24/31	25	26	27	28	29	30

AUGUST

S	M	Tu	W	Th	F	S
	1	2	3	4	5	6
7	8	9	10	11	12	13
14	15	16	17	18	19	20
21	22	23	24	25	26	27
28	29	30				

SEPTEMBER

S	M	Tu	W	Th	F	S
				1	2	3
4	5	6	7	8	9	10
11	12	13	14	15	16	17
18	19	20	21	22	23	24
25	26	27	28	29	30	

OCTOBER

S	M	Tu	W	Th	F	S
						1
2	3	4	5	6	7	8
9	10	11	12	13	14	15
16	17	18	19	20	21	22
23/30	24/31	25	26	27	28	29

NOVEMBER

S	M	Tu	W	Th	F	S
		1	2	3	4	5
6	7	8	9	10	11	12
13	14	15	16	17	18	19
20	21	22	23	24	25	26
27	28	29	30			

DECEMBER

S	M	Tu	W	Th	F	S
				1	2	3
4	5	6	7	8	9	10
11	12	13	14	15	16	17
18	19	20	21	22	23	24
25	26	27	28	29	30	31

A Look at the calendar. Answer the questions.

1. What day of the week is the 13th of January?   ………………

2. What day of the week is the 4th of May?   ………………

3. What day of the week is the 20th of November?   ………………

4. What day of the week is the 11th of October?   ………………

5. Which month has Thursday, the 30th?   ………………

6. Which months have the first day on a Saturday?   ………………………

7. Which months have Monday, the 11th?   ………………………

8. Which month has twenty-eight days?   ………………

B Listen to the first ten days of January, and to the months of the year. Repeat, if you like.

6 There are two secretaries in the office

Study the examples.

Singular	Plural	Singular	Plural
a waiter	two waiters	a waitress	three waitresses
a secretary	four secretaries	a man	five men

Write the plurals for these words.

1. a teacher   two ....
2. an actor   three ....
3. an accountant   four ....
4. an actress   five ....
5. a dictionary   two ....
6. a woman   six ....

7. a doctor   many ....
8. a dentist   three ....
9. a guess   three ....
10. a businessman   six ....
11. a cross   two ....
12. a parent   two ....

7 Is this your office?

A Match the drawings with the words in the box.

we	you	I	he	they	you	she

B Complete the dialogue. Use the words in the box.

1. MARA: Is this your company's office, Dana?

2. DANA: Yes, it's .... new office. Isn't it nice?

3. MARA: And is this your computer?

4. DANA: No, it isn't. It belongs to Jim Ross, our manager. It's .... computer.

5. MARA: Oh, what nice plants on the window!

6. DANA: Well, they're not my plants. There's a new secretary, too, called Jane. They're .... plants.

7. MARA: And this is your table, isn't it?

8. DANA: Er, no, it's not. The two typists work there. It's .... table.

9. MARA: Where's .... desk, then?

10. DANA: Er, well, there isn't a desk for me, really. But here's .... chair, in the corner. Nice, isn't it?

her	his	our	your	my	their

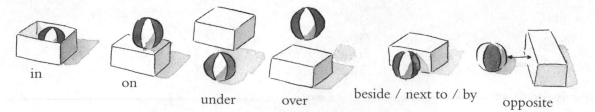

in   on   under   over   beside / next to / by   opposite

📼 **Listen and tick the right picture. Complete the answers.**

Example: *Where's the pen? It's on the book.*
Where?
On the book, on the table, by the window.

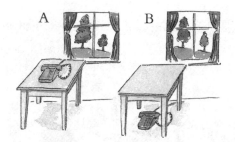

A   B

1. Where's the phone?

It's *on the table, by the window* .

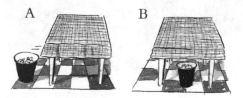

A   B

2. Where's the bin?

It's ....

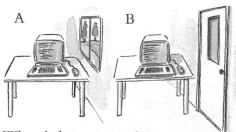

A   B

3. Where's the computer?

It's ....

A   B

4. Where are the books?

They're ....

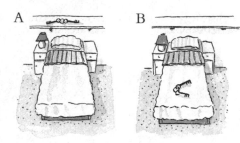

A   B

5. Where are the keys?

They're ....

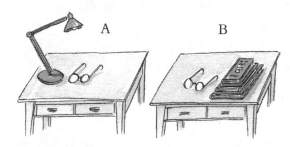

A   B

6. Where are my glasses?

They're ....

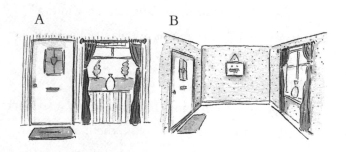

A   B

7. Where's the window?

It's ....

If you like, listen again and repeat for rhythm practice.

1

FINDING OUT

1 What's the long form?

Write the long form for the underlined words.

Example: _What's_ your name? ..What is..

1. My <u>name's</u> Jenny. ....
2. <u>Where's</u> the pen? ....
3. <u>It's</u> on the table. ....
4. <u>I'm</u> Kari. ....
5. <u>He's</u> John. ....

6. <u>She's</u> a teacher. ....
7. <u>We're</u> in the coffee shop. ....
8. <u>They're</u> plumbers. ....
9. There <u>isn't</u> a lift. ....
10. There <u>aren't</u> any public telephones. ....

2 What's your name?

Read the answers. Write the questions.

Example: Q: _What's your name?_
A: _My name's Jim._

1. Q: ....?
   A: No, I'm not Maria. I'm Pat.
2. Q: ....?
   A: Yes, I'm a journalist.
3. Q: ....?
   A: I'm from Canada.
4. Q: ....?
   A: It's 23, Long Road, Bellevue, Ontario.

5. Q: ....?
   A: The painting is in the room on the top floor.
6. Q: ....?
   A: No, I'm sorry, there isn't a coffee shop in this building.
7. Q: ....?
   A: Yes, there are two public telephones on the first floor.

3 How many doors are there?

What's in your language classroom – or your office?
Write a description from memory. Answer the questions.

Next time you are there, check your answers. Is your memory good?

In my classroom (_or_ In my office),

(_How many windows are there?_)   There .... window(s).
(_How many doors are there?_)   There .... door(s).
(_How many tables are there?_)   There .... table(s).
(_How many chairs are there?_)   There .... chair(s).
(_How many telephones are there?_)   There .... telephone(s).
(_How many computers are there?_)   There .... computer(s).

There's also ....   There are also ....

A Match each word in column 1 with a word in column 2.

Column 1	Column 2
1. coffee	light
2. public	desk
3. first	spaces
4. parking	floor
5. information	telephones
6. natural	shop

B Write the words in the box below in one of the four columns. Some words can go into more than one column.

1. In a room at home	2. In a room at work	3. In a building	4. Outside

> a radio   a television   a chair   a table   a window   a lift   stairs
> an information desk   public telephones   a coffee shop   parking spaces
> a computer

Choose a word from the box below. Write a sentence about each person.

Example:

He's a waiter.

She's a waitress.

1. He's a ....

2. She's a ....

3. He's a ....

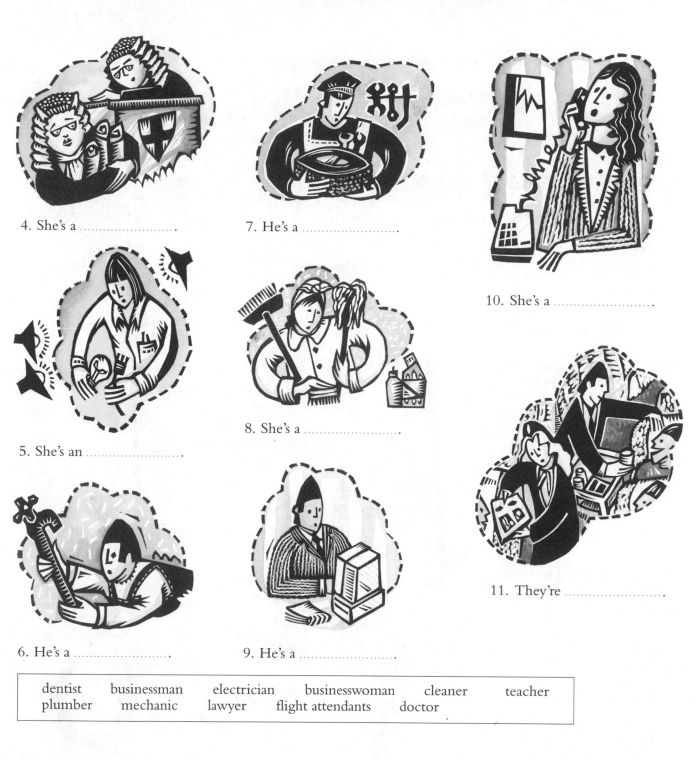

4. She's a ....

7. He's a ....

10. She's a ....

5. She's an ....

8. She's a ....

6. He's a ....

9. He's a ....

11. They're ....

dentist	businessman	electrician	businesswoman	cleaner	teacher
plumber	mechanic	lawyer	flight attendants	doctor	

6 Numbers

A 🔲 Listen and tick the numbers you hear. The first one is an example.

1. 13 ☑   30 ☐
2. 14 ☐   40 ☐
3. 15 ☐   50 ☐
4. 16 ☐   60 ☐

B 🔲 Listen and tick the words you hear.

1. a meal ☐   a mill ☐   a meat ☐
2. brake fast ☐   breakfast ☐   brick fast ☐
3. We are about ☐   Whereabouts? ☐   Where are the boats? ☐
4. tanks ☐   thinks ☐   thanks ☐
5. It's half past nine ☐   It's half past five ☐   It's half past eight ☐
6. Exercise 2 on page 17 ☐   Exercise 2E on page 70 ☐   Exercise 2E on page 17 ☐

C 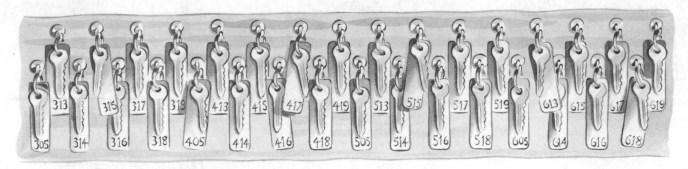 You are a receptionist. Listen and choose a key for each speaker.

1. Speaker 1 .... 2. Speaker 2 .... 3. Speaker 3 .... 4. Speaker 4 ....

---

7 Directory enquiries

A Listen to some telephone enquiries. Fill in the missing information. Correct the incorrect codes. What is the code for your country?

Country Codes

Algeria		Indonesia	62
	213	Mexico	52
Australia	61	Portugal	351
Brazil	55	Saudi Arabia	966
the Czech Republic	42	Spain	34
Dominica		Thailand	56
Egypt	20	UK	44
Finland		USA	1
France	33	Zimbabwe	263
Greece	30		

B Now listen to these telephone enquiries. Fill in the missing information.

NAME   ADDRESS   TEL.

Darby   26 Rutland Ave   695 7309

Minneapolis

Burns House

NAME   ADDRESS

---

8 Where do you come from?

A Listen to people meeting each other at a hotel. Fill in the missing information.

Conversation 1

1. Paula meets ....

2. Arturo comes from ....

Conversation 2

3. Brenda meets Sita ....

4. Sita is from ....

Conversation 3

5. Arturo meets ....

6. He is from ....

7. Arturo's parents come from

....

B Now listen and reply.

Unit 1 FINDING OUT

9 Describing a painting

Describe the painting.

This is a picture of .... and

.... In the sitting room

there is ....

and .... There's also ....

and ....

.... On the floor

there is .... On the walls there

are ....and

....

 Listen to a description of the painting. Is it the same as yours? What is different?

10 English teacher required

A ▤ Read these ads for jobs. Use a dictionary to help you.

> **ENGLISH TEACHER**
> required for small language
> school. No evening work,
> regular hours, good holidays.
> Interesting work.

> **Gardener**
> required for large
> country home.
> Weekends only.
> Modern equipment.

> **Part-time translator**
> required for large
> petrochemical
> company. Work at
> home in your free time.
> Good pay.

Match the jobs and the kind of work.

Example: *work for a small company* _teacher_

1. no work after 6 pm. ....
2. work from Monday to Friday ....
3. work on Saturday and Sunday ....
4. work for a family ....
5. work for a large company ....
6. work outside ....

B Now write an advertisement for one other job.

Example: *Secretary required …*

....

....

Show your advertisements to your teacher, if you like.

11 Visual dictionary

Complete the visual dictionary for Unit 1 on page 126.

WHAT HAVE YOU GOT?

1 I've got a dictionary

A What have you got to help you learn English?
Write *Yes, I have* or *No, I haven't* in column 1. Write the number of things you have in column 2.

Example: *Have you got a dictionary?*
Column 1: write *Yes, I have* or *No, I haven't.*
How many have you got?
Column 2: write *1* or *2* or *3*.

	Column 1	Column 2	Column 3
	Have you got ...?	*How many have you got?*	*How many has the speaker got?*
1. a coursebook?	....	I've got	....
2. a notebook?	....	I've got	....
3. a dictionary?	....	I've got	....
4. a cassette recorder?	....	I've got	....
5. a computer?	....	I've got	....
6. a video recorder?	....	I've got	....
7. any magazines in English?	....	I've got	....
8. any books in English?	....	I've got	....
9. any newspapers in English?	....	I've got	....

B ▭ Listen to a person answering the questions. Fill in column 3.
Listen to the questions again. This time, give your own answers.

2 *To have*

Complete the long and short forms of *to have*.

Long forms	*Short forms*
1. I have got	I've got
2. You .... got	You've ....
3. .... has got	He's got
4. She has got	............'s got
5. It	It'...... got
6. We have	............'ve ....
7.	They'............

The long form of *have* is used at the beginning of questions, and in short answers.

Example: *Have you got any books?*
Yes, I have. (**not** ~~*Yes, I've.*~~)

3 Have you got any plants?

Study the examples.

A: *Have you got a video recorder?*   B: *No, but I've got a radio.*
A: *Have you got any books in English?*   B: *No, I haven't got any.*
A: *I've got some books in English and some books in Bulgarian.*

Now add *a*, *any* or *some* in the sentences.

1. Have you got .... friends in other countries, Julie?

2. Well, I've got .... pen friend in Kampala, and I've got .... cousins in Jamaica.

3. What have you got in that big briefcase? Have you got .... pen?

4. I've got .... computer, ... notebook, ... newspapers, and ... let's

   see, ... pens and .... pencil.

5. Have you got .... plants in the bathroom?

6. No, I haven't got .... at all in the bathroom. But I've got .... plants in the
   bedroom, and I've got lots in the kitchen.

4 Mary and John have got two sons

Look at the family tree and complete the sentences.

1. Mary and John have got two sons, Paul and ....

2. Susan's the daughter of .... and ....

3. Michael and .... have got a sister, ...

4. Michael's the husband of ....

5. Susan and Michael have got a brother, ...

6. James has got a mother, ...

7. Lucy has got a father, ...

8. James and Lucy have two grandparents, ... and ....

9. Mary and John have three children, Susan, ... and Michael, and two

   grandchildren, ... and Lucy.

5 Sentence rhythm

▭ Listen to this conversation and repeat
What have you got? **each time you hear it.**

FLIGHT ATTENDANT: A drink for you?
PASSENGER: What have you got?
FLIGHT ATTENDANT: We've got coffee, tea, orange
             juice or mineral water.
PASSENGER: Coffee, please.

Now listen again.
It's your turn to ask and answer.
Say *What have you got?* **and choose**
something: a drink, an ice cream
and a newspaper.

Example: *Coffee, please.* or *Tea, please.*

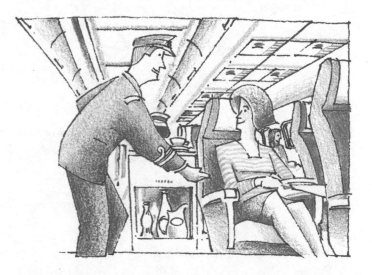

6 I've got a brother and two sisters

A Which of the words in the box are for men only? Women only? Men or women? Put them in the correct column.

Men only	Women only	Men or women
....	....	....
....	....	....
....	....	....
....	....	....

> parent   husband   sister
> grandparent   daughter   cousin
> friend   mother   son
> wife   brother   father

B 🔲 Listen to four speakers. Put *1, 2, 3* and *4* under the right diagrams.

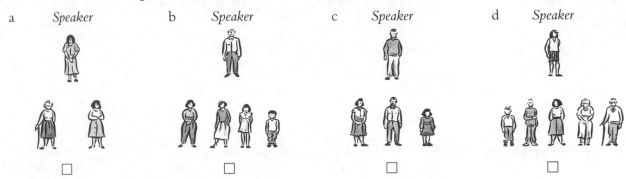

a *Speaker*   b *Speaker*   c *Speaker*   d *Speaker*

□   □   □   □

What family have you got? Complete the sentence.

I've got ....

7 What have you got in your pocket?

A What have you got in your pocket, briefcase, handbag or desk? Make a list.

....

B 🔲 Listen to two people. Write a number next to each thing they've got, 1 for the first thing mentioned on the recording, 2 for the second, etc.

Speaker 1   *Speaker 2*

C 🔲 Now listen again and write the missing words.

1. I've got a .... of string.

2. I've got some handkerchiefs – .... ones.

3. I've got .... in the pockets of my trousers because I've got a rather large .... in them.

4. In the pockets of my cardigan, I've got a .... tissue.

A What have you got in your bedroom? Tick the items.

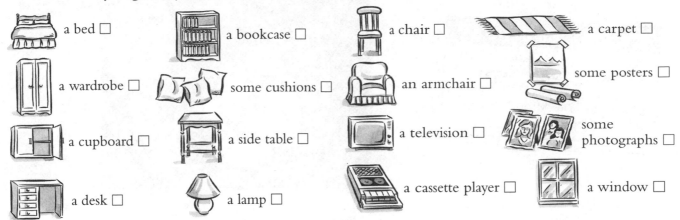

a bed ☐   a bookcase ☐   a chair ☐   a carpet ☐

a wardrobe ☐   some cushions ☐   an armchair ☐   some posters ☐

a cupboard ☐   a side table ☐   a television ☐   some photographs ☐

a desk ☐   a lamp ☐   a cassette player ☐   a window ☐

B Here are three descriptions of bedrooms. Read the descriptions and match each to a plan.

1. My room is at the end of the corridor. On my door there is a small bell. My room's got a big bed, with a nice yellow bedspread. My bed is in front of the window. When you look out of the window you can see the garden of our house, and the primary school of Oyak.

   Next to the bed there is a small table. On the table, there is a lamp. There is a chair behind the table. On the wall near the door I've got photographs of my family and friends. There are also photos of children, because I love children.

   Near the table there is a cupboard, for my clothes. Behind the door is a bookcase. But there are no books! On the shelves, I've got some plants, a small clock and a radio.

   The room is small but comfortable. I feel relaxed in my room. (Sema)

2. Opposite the door, there are four cupboards along the wall. Then, on the right, against the wall, I've got a working desk with three shelves above it, full of books and my tape recorder and cassettes.

   On the left, there is my classical guitar hanging on the wall, next to the bed. I've got a television too, on a cupboard beside the desk. On the opposite wall there is a window and a bookcase.

   There is a side table beside my bed. There is a small lamp on the table. The walls everywhere have got a lot of pictures and posters. (Julio)

3. My room is small, but lovely. The carpet on the floor is very colourful. On the right I've got my cassette player and on the left, my wardrobe. Next to the cassette player there is a table and then some bookshelves. The table has got a lamp on it. On the left, beside the wardrobe, I've got my bed with cushions on it. Next to the bed there is a small armchair with cushions, too. I've got a vase of flowers on the bedside table which is between the armchair and the wardrobe.

   The walls are white and covered with posters. I haven't got a dressing table, only a mirror on the wall. The curtains at the window are colourful – they match the carpet.

   My favourite thing is the balcony, which is lovely on long, hot summer nights. (Mihaela)

a

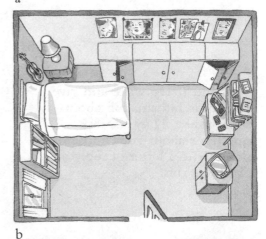

b

c

Read the advertisement for a house swap.

SWAP HOUSES?

Our house is free in January. It's next to the beach in Westport. Sleeps 6. All modern conveniences. Write to: Suni and Barry De Millo, Box 61, Palmerston, New Zealand

Here is a letter asking Suni and Barry some questions about their house. Complete the gaps and add one or two questions.

Dear Suni and Barry,

Your house next to the beach sounds great! Can I ask a few questions about it?

Has it got a large kitchen? Is there a fridge? How many bedrooms has it got? How many .... has it got? Is there a .... for the car? Have you got a television?

....?

....?

I'm sorry to ask so many questions! I hope to hear from you soon.

Goodbye for now,

.... (your name)

Suni and Barry write and give you some information about their house. They also ask questions about your house or flat. Write a letter of reply. Start like this.

Dear Suni and Barry,

Thank you for your letter and all the answers about your house. Here is some information about my house to help you.

....

....

....

....

....

See you soon,

....

Show your letters to your teacher, if you like.

10 Visual dictionary

Complete the visual dictionary for Unit 2 on page 127.

3

WHAT WOULD YOU LIKE TO EAT?

▭ **Complete the information.**

Example: *one packet*   *two packets*

1. one carton   two ....   6. one ....   seven apples

2. one tin   three ....   7. one ....   eight potatoes

3. one .... four boxes   8. one tomato   nine ....

4. one bottle   five ....   9. one ....   ten carrots

5. one .... six eggs   10. one ....   eleven chocolates

Some things are counted.

Example: *one egg, two eggs, three eggs*

The nouns for these things are called *countable nouns*.

Some things are not counted.

Example: *some sugar* (**not** ~~one sugar~~, ~~two sugars~~)

The nouns for these things are called *uncountable nouns*.

A Put the nouns in the box under the right heading.

Countable nouns   Uncountable nouns

apple	sugar	rice	water	milk	spaghetti	banana	money
wine	cheese	bean	pea	grape	noodles	chocolate	toast
cake	biscuit	cereal	butter	lamb	beef	yoghurt	bottle
fruit juice	bread	soup	orange				

B Look at these examples.

1. *a banana* (countable):
   I'd like a banana, please.
   I'd like four bananas, please.
   I'd like some bananas, please.
   There's a banana on the table.
   There are bananas in the shops.

2. *rice* (uncountable):
   some rice (**not** ~~one rice~~, ~~two rices~~)
   I'd like some rice, please.
   There's rice in the shops today. (**not** ~~there are rice ...~~)

Complete the sentences.

1. With countable nouns, use *a* or *an*, numbers (*one, two* ...) or ....

2. With .... nouns, use no article or ....

A Add the missing names.

rice   cheese   peas   milk   1. ....   2. ....   fruit juice

wine   3. ....   noodles   spaghetti   soup   chocolates   4. ....

            5. ....   tomatoes   beans   grapes   6. ....

B Put these foods into the right containers for your country.

packets: ....

cartons: ....

boxes: ....

tins: ....

bottles: ....

bags: ....

C 📭 Listen and compare your answers with the speakers'. What food comes in these containers?

In America:

1. in plastic bags: ....

2. in paper cartons: ....

3. wrapped in cellophane: ....

In Malaysia:

4. in your own bag, at the market: ....

5. in bottles: ....

6. in packets: ....

7. in boxes: ....

In Northern Ireland:

 8. in cartons: ....

 9. in bottles: ....

10. in tins: ....

11. in a packet at the supermarket:

....

12. in a brown paper bag at the greengrocer's:

....

A These sentences have all got some mistakes. How many foods can you add from the box below to make correct sentences?

Example: *I'd like a dozen soup, please.* (**incorrect**)
I'd like a dozen eggs, tomatoes, oranges, etc. (**correct**)

1. I'd like a kilo of milk, please.

....

2. I'd like a tin of wine.

....

3. I'd like a bottle of eggs.

....

4. I'd like a litre of tomatoes.

....

5. I'd like a box of fish, please.

....

6. I'd like half a kilo of mineral water.

....

7. I'd like half a litre of chocolates.

....

eggs	milk	tomatoes	oranges	chocolates	potatoes	beans
apples	rice	carrots	fish	soup	wine	orange juice	peas
mineral water	noodles	cheese	grapes	bananas		

B 📼 Listen to some possible answers.

---

5 Stress and intonation   pronunciation

A 📼 Look at these sentences and listen to them on the recording. Repeat them, if you like.

1. What would you like?   I'd like a tin of peas, please.
   I'd like ● ● ● ● , please.
2. What would you like?   I'd like a kilo of peas, please.
   I'd like ● ●● ● ● , please.
3. What would you like?   I'd like a box of noodles, please.
   I'd like ● ● ● ● ● , please.
4. What would you like?   I'd like a kilo of noodles, please.
   I'd like ● ●● ● ● ● , please.

B 📼 Listen to ten sentences. Fill in the missing words.

1. I'd like a tin of ...., please.
2. I'd like a tin of carrots, please.
3. I'd like a bottle of wine, please.
4. I'd like a carton of ...., please.
5. I'd like a packet of ...., please.
6. I'd like a kilo of peas, please.
7. I'd like a .... of ...., please.
8. I'd like a box of ...., please.
9. I'd like a .... of ...., please.
10. I'd like a .... of ...., please.

C What is the rhythm pattern for these words?

1. tomatoes   ......
2. potatoes   ......
3. bananas   ......
4. spaghetti   ......

   a. ●●●   b. ●●●   c. ●●●

6 How much is this?

A Look at these examples.

How much is this?   *How much are these?*   *How much is that?*   *How much are those?*

B ⟺ Listen to these short conversations. Tick the word you hear.

1. this ☐ that ☐ these ☐ those ☐   6. this ☐ that ☐ these ☐ those ☐
2. this ☐ that ☐ these ☐ those ☐   7. this ☐ that ☐ these ☐ those ☐
3. this ☐ that ☐ these ☐ those ☐   8. this ☐ that ☐ these ☐ those ☐
4. this ☐ that ☐ these ☐ those ☐   9. this ☐ that ☐ these ☐ those ☐
5. this ☐ that ☐ these ☐ those ☐

C ⟺ Listen again. Which of these food items are in the shop? Tick them.

apples ☐   tomatoes ☐   wine ☐   mineral water ☐   potatoes ☐   cheese ☐   pineapple ☐
bananas ☐   oranges ☐   rice ☐   yoghurt ☐   orange juice ☐   grapes ☐

⟺ Listen again and check. How many of the things on the list have you got at home?

7 I like Indian food

A ⟺ Listen to three people from Western countries talking about their favourite foods from Asia. Tick the kinds of food they mention.

1. curry ☐
2. currants ☐
3. vegetable curry ☐
4. tabouli ☐
5. Indian food ☐

6. rice ☐
7. Vietnamese food ☐
8. Chinese food ☐
9. fish ☐

10. Thai food ☐
11. noodles ☐
12. vegetables ☐
13. vegetarian ☐

B Which of the foods are your favourites too? Write down some of your favourite foods in the first column. How many are from other countries?

My favourite foods   *My parents' favourite foods*

....

....

Now list some of your parents' favourite foods. Are they local or traditional foods – or foods from other countries?

C Is your diet different from your parents'? Complete one of these sentences:

My favourite foods are ...., and these are also my parents' favourite foods.

My favourite foods are ...., but my parents' favourites are

....

A Read these five sentences. Use a dictionary if you need help.

1. From a visit to three Asian countries, one thing is clear: the Asian diet is now more Westernised.
2. Asian supermarkets now have a long list of Western foods.
3. At a supermarket in Ampang Park, Kuala Lumpur, there is a shelf, four metres long, for milk in tins.
4. In one Bangkok supermarket there are more than a dozen different brands of milk drinks.
5. Unfortunately, there are now more Western diet-related diseases.

B The five sentences are from an article called 'Asian food'. What is the article about? Tick *a* or *b*.

1. a. food in the West ☐   b. Western food in Asia ☐
2. a. milk products ☐   b. Kuala Lumpur ☐
3. a. diseases in the West ☐   b. diseases from Western food ☐

C Check your answers on page 162. Then read the whole article.

From a visit to three Asian countries, one thing is clear: the Asian diet is now more Westernised. The traditional Asian food – eaten three times a day – is rice. But now there are also meals of wheat products, such as toast for breakfast, and milk products.

Asian supermarkets now have a long list of Western foods such as breads, cakes and biscuits, snack foods, tinned goods and fizzy soft-drinks, pasta (wheat noodles), breakfast cereals, butter, cheese, lamb and beef.

But most striking is the large number of milk products. Milk products traditionally aren't part of an Asian diet – many Asians are actually allergic to milk. But there are now ads on television for milk. Milk, according to the ads, is 'modern', middle class and healthy. At a supermarket in Ampang Park, Kuala Lumpur, there is a shelf, four metres long, for milk in tins.

In one Bangkok supermarket there are more than a dozen different brands of milk drinks, from strawberry to pineapple flavour. In a typical supermarket in Chiang Mai in northern Thailand (population 1.2 million), there is fresh milk, and flavoured long-life milk in mini cartons. There are also fruit yoghurts in pineapple, orange and lychee flavours.

Unfortunately, there are now more Western diet-related diseases.

D List the Western foods in the text that are popular in some Asian supermarkets.

....

E About you and your country.

Is milk popular in your country? ....

Which milk products are popular in your country? List them.

....

9 Visual dictionary

Complete the visual dictionary for Unit 3 on page 127.

A SENSE OF COLOUR

| 1 Where do you buy your socks? | present simple questions |

📼 Listen to the questions and answer them. Use the expressions in the box to help you.

1.

....

4.

....

2.

....

5.

....

3.

....

6.

....

from a clothes shop   from a department store   from Luigi's (name of shop)
at the market   from (or at) the supermarket   every day   once a month
twice a year   never

| 2 Where does he buy his socks? | 1st and 3rd person verbs |

Match the questions and answers, then complete the answers.

1. Where does he buy his shirts?
2. Where does she buy her blouses?
3. Where do they buy their trousers?
4. Where do you buy your jackets?
5. Where do your friends buy their skirts?
6. How often do you buy flowers?
7. How often does Mary give roses?
8. How often does Paolo receive books?
9. How often do they buy chocolates?
10. How often does your teacher sing songs?

a. They never .... chocolates.
b. Well, Maria and Dara .... their skirts at the market.
c. He .... them from a department store.
d. Oh, she always .... at the end of the class.
e. She .... her mother roses once a year.
f. She .... them from the market.
g. He .... books once a month, by post.
h. I .... them from a shop in the town centre.
i. I never .... flowers.
j. They .... them from Luigi's.

A ▤ Make sure you understand the verb *prefer*. Use your dictionary.

▱ Listen and answer questions about clothes and coffee. Answer *brown, black, white* or *blue*. Listen to the example first.

B ▱ Think of one of your friends. Listen and answer questions about her or him.

C Now complete the questions and write your answers. You can listen again if you like.

1. Q: .... you prefer blue or ....?
   A: ....

2. Q: .... you prefer your coffee black or ....?
   A: ....

3. Q: .... black T-shirts or .... ones?
   A: ....

4. Q: .... your friend .... or .... jeans?
   A: ....

5. Q: .... your friend prefer .... or .... ?
   A: ....

6. Q: .... your ....-............ or white ....?
   A: ....

Write in the colour words.

red	green	blue	grey	black	pink	yellow	gold	brown	orange

1. a .... flamingo

2. a .... cat

3. an .... traffic light

4. a .... cloud

5. .... sky

6. a .... dog

7. a .... fire

8. a .... ring

9. .... grass

10. a .... lemon

▱ Listen and check your answers.

A Match the pictures and the words. Number 1 is an example.

a. a blouse	d. a coat	g. a hat	j. a jacket	m. a pair of shorts	p. a pair of socks
b. a woman's suit	e. a tie	h. a pair of jeans	k. a skirt	n. a sweater	q. a shirt
c. a pair of shoes	f. a pair of tights	i. a raincoat	l. a dress	o. a scarf	r. a pair of trousers

B 📖 Find the words *fashionable*, *conventional* and *comfortable* in the dictionary. Now answer the questions about clothes in your country. Tick the boxes.

FASHION QUESTIONNAIRE

❶ What colours are fashionable in
your country this year?

....

❷ At work, do people prefer
☐ a. conventional clothes?
☐ b. fashionable clothes?
☐ c. comfortable clothes?

❸ On holiday, do people prefer
☐ a. conventional clothes?
☐ b. fashionable clothes?
☐ c. comfortable clothes?

❹ Are suits in your country
☐ a. fashionable?
☐ b. conventional?

❺ Do men and women in your
country prefer
☐ a. fashionable shoes?
☐ b. comfortable shoes?

C 📼 Listen to two people answering the questions. What are their answers?

Woman 1. ....
         2. a. ☐   b. ☐   c. ☐
         3. a. ☐   b. ☐   c. ☐
         4. a. ☐   b. ☐
         5. a. ☐   b. ☐

Man 1. ....
      2. a. ☐   b. ☐   c. ☐
      3. a. ☐   b. ☐   c. ☐
      4. a. ☐   b. ☐
      5. a. ☐   b. ☐

A Read the sentences. Guess what words are missing.

1. My jackets are made in Japan. They're made of ....

2. Your blouses are made in Brazil. They're made of ....

3. His ties are made in Thailand. They're made of ....

4. Her skirts are made in Scotland. They're made of ....

5. Our raincoats are made in Romania. They're made of ....

6. Their shirts are made in Sri Lanka. They're made of ....

B 📼 Listen to the sentences on the recording and check your guesses. Write the words you hear. Then listen again and repeat the sentences. Pay attention to the rhythm.

7 The colours of my country

7 The colours of my country

A Think about the colours of your country – colours of the countryside, your flag, colours of buildings, colours of flowers …

Write some colours in the boxes for *My country*.

	a. Colours of the countryside	b. Colours of flowers	c. Colours of the flag	d. Colours of buildings
1. My country				
2. Country A				
3. Country B				

B ☐☐ Listen to two people talking about colours in their countries.

Put the colours mentioned by the first speaker in the boxes for *Country A*. Put the colours mentioned by the second speaker in the boxes for *Country B*. Can you guess their countries?

8 Jeans give self-confidence

A What do you know about jeans? Answer these questions.

1. What are jeans made of? ....

2. Which country do they come from? ....

Think about these questions.

Are jeans popular in your country? Why or why not?
Do you think jeans are for work or for weekends and holidays?
Do you think that jeans are part of 'designer fashion' – or high fashion?

B ▬ **Make sure you understand these words.**

a uniform   relaxed   self-confidence   an individual   a survey

Read this article about jeans quickly. Find the answers to the two questions in Part A. Do the exercises after the article, check your answers, then read the article again.

THE WESTERN UNIFORM

People don't write a lot about jeans. But one in two men and four in ten women under the age of 45 buy at least one pair each year. That's a lot of denim! We are used to this Western uniform, and we don't stop to think how amazing it is for one piece of clothing to be popular in so many countries, and with so many people.

A recent survey gave the main reasons for wearing jeans: they are comfortable, relaxed, and look good on most people. But is this really true? Stand on any street corner. You can see that some men and women wear jeans even though they don't look good in them. They feel all right about it, because jeans give self-confidence. Other clothes are comfortable and relaxed, but jeans have something special.

Jeans come from nineteenth-century American workclothes. But they are now part of designer fashion. As one designer explains, 'Jeans are never out of fashion. They are always around. Jeans are popular because they don't say anything about fashion. They say a lot about you.' So jeans are a uniform, but they make every individual feel special.

C What is the meaning of these expressions? Choose _a_ or _b_.

1. People buy at least one pair of jeans each year.
   a. People buy one pair each year. ☐
   b. People buy one pair or more each year. ☐
2. We are used to this uniform.
   a. We know this uniform very well. ☐
   b. We wear this uniform. ☐
3. We don't stop to think how amazing it is.
   a. We forget that it is amazing. ☐
   b. We always think that it is amazing. ☐
4. They wear jeans even though they don't look good in them.
   a. They wear jeans because jeans look good. ☐
   b. They know they don't look good in jeans, but they feel all right about it. ☐
5. Jeans say a lot about you.
   a. People talk a lot about jeans. ☐
   b. Your jeans show what kind of a person you are. ☐

D What do you think about jeans? Tick the answer that shows your ideas.

Do you wear jeans?   Yes, I do. ☐   No, I don't. ☐
Are jeans your favourite clothes?   Yes, they are. ☐   No, they aren't. ☐
Do you prefer blue jeans or black jeans?   blue jeans ☐   black jeans ☐

9 A raincoat is essential in summer or winter

A Read these two paragraphs about essential clothes in two different countries.

Visiting Ireland in the summer? Bring light clothes for the sunny days of course, but don't forget your sweater and a hat and coat or jacket for rainy days. In Ireland, a raincoat is essential in summer or winter, because there's a lot of rain. A sweater is essential too, because it's often cold. And strong shoes are good for the country.

In California, a hat is essential in summer, because there's so much sun. It's good to have loose clothing because of the heat. People wear shorts and light clothes even in cities. In some parts, the evenings are cool and a light jacket or sweater is a good thing to have.

B Write a paragraph about your country.

In .... (your country) .... (and ....) is (are) essential (in the summer / the winter) because …

It's good to have .... because …

....

....

....

10 Visual dictionary

Complete the visual dictionary for Unit 4 on page 128.

Unit 4 A SENSE OF COLOUR

GOOD HABITS, NEW ROUTINES?

1 Why does he go shopping in the market?

A There are two questions for each answer. Find the right endings for each question in the box below.

1. Q: What time do you ....?

   or What time do you ....?

   A: Oh, never before 8 am.

2. Q: How often do you ....?

   or How often do you ....?

   A: Erm … usually three times a day.

3. Q: How often do you ....?

   or How often do you ....?

   A: Once a year, to a cottage by the sea.

4. Q: Why does he ....?

   or Why does he ....?

   A: Because he likes the spices.

5. Q: What does she ....?

   or Why does she ....?

   A: She watches the news.

go shopping in the market	have a meal	cook curry	do at nine
know so much	have a cup of tea	get up in the morning	leave the house
go on holiday	go away		

▭ Listen to the questions and check your answers.

B Write a second question for the answer.

1. Q: Does he do the cooking? *or* ....?

   A: Only when his wife is ill.

2. Q: Does she go out a lot? *or* ....?

   A: Only when her husband is away.

3. Q: Where do you buy vegetables? *or* ....?

   A: Oh, the supermarket, always.

C ▭ Listen to some possible questions. Compare your questions with the ones you hear.

Match the words on the left with the appropriate words from the box on the right.
Look at the example first.

Example: *get dressed*

get ....

have ....

listen to ....

have a ....

go to ....

watch ....

tidy ....

read ....

wash ....

go ....

make ....

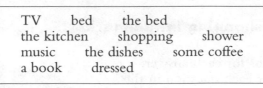

TV	bed	the bed
the kitchen	shopping	shower
music	the dishes	some coffee
a book	dressed	

3 I always look, and she always listens present simple

Study these examples of the present simple tense in English.

I You We They	have. eat. listen. look. go. kiss. push. watch.	He She It	has. eats. listens. looks. goes. kisses. pushes. watches.

	LONG FORM				LONG FORM	
I You We They	do not	eat. go. watch.	He She It	does not	eat. go. watch.
	SHORT FORM				SHORT FORM	
	don't	eat. go. watch.		doesn't	eat. go. watch.

Complete these rules for verbs in the present simple.

1. *I, you, we* and *they* use the main form of the verb.

2. *He* or *she*: for most verbs, add ....

3. For verbs ending in *o, ss, ch* or *sh*, add ....

To have does not follow the rules. The forms for *to have* are:

4. I or you ....

5. She or he ....

Choose a day in an ordinary week. Read the expressions, and add a few more to the list. Write some of them on the time line, to show when you do these things.

go to bed	go for a walk	have lunch	leave the house	watch TV
go shopping	have breakfast	wake up	get dressed	read the newspaper
have a shower	tidy up the room	go to work	listen to music	

....

....

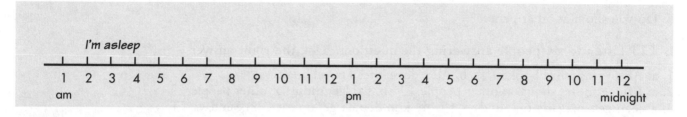

Now write another time line for one of these days.

a holiday   another person's day (a friend, or someone in your family)   a perfect day

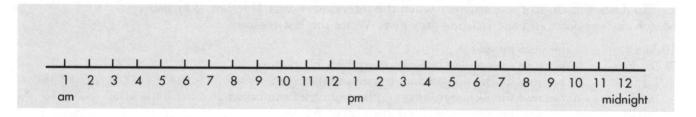

A Here are some verbs from Unit 5.

get up	get dressed	wake up	sing	lie	talk	start
read	watch	tidy up	wash up	sleep	learn	use
write	go	stand				

To help you remember them, write a short sentence or expression with each verb.

Example: *I go to work on the bus. I wash up after the meal.*

Then put as many expressions as you can into these categories.

I do this in the morning: ....

I do this in the afternoon: ....

I do this in the evening: ....

I do this at home: ....

I do this at work: ....

I never do this: ....

Other category (write one of your own): ....

B Here are some more verbs from the unit. Put them into categories, or add something beside each one to help you remember: for example, a drawing, the meaning in English or the meaning in your own language.

leave (the house)   smoke   listen   kiss   say   make   shake (hands)

6 Do you read travel books?

A Write answers to these questions. (Be honest!)

Write *Yes, I always do* (or *I sometimes do*, or *I often do*, or *I usually do*). Or: *No, I don't*
(or *No, never*).

1. Do you get up early on Sundays? ....

2. Do you eat fast food (for example pizza or burgers)? ....

3. Do you tidy your house or flat every day? ....

4. Do you spend a lot of money when you are on holiday? ....

5. Do you read travel books? ....

6. Do you shout at other people? ....

B 🔲 Listen to six people answering the questions. Tick the right answer.

1. a. Alex reads travel books. ☐   b. Alex doesn't read travel books. ☐
2. a. Bridget never shouts at other people. ☐   b. Bridget shouts at other people. ☐
3. a. Joan gets up early on Sundays. ☐   b. Joan doesn't get up early on Sundays. ☐
4. a. Rod never spends very much on holidays. ☐   b. Rod probably spends quite a lot. ☐
5. a. Nick doesn't tidy his flat every day. ☐   b. Nick usually tidies his flat every day. ☐
6. a. Ned doesn't eat fast food. ☐   b. Ned eats fast food. ☐

C 🔲 Listen again to their answers when the interviewer asks *Why?* or *Why not?*
Match the speakers and the reasons they give. Write the last reason.

1. Alex   a. because he's lazy
2. Bridget   b. because she's a very bad-tempered, horrible person
3. Joan   c. because it's the only chance to laze about
4. Rod   d. because she likes travelling to other countries and books give her some ideas
5. Nick   e. because he goes skiing, and that's expensive

6. Ned (write the reason): ....

7 He finds murderers!

A When you go to someone's house for the first time, what things do you look at?
The furniture? The pictures on the walls? The colours? Make a list.

When I go to someone's house for the first time, I look at:

....

....

**What do those things tell
you about that person?**

B Look at these pictures
about a murder. Match the
words and the pictures.

a medical examiner
the ceiling
a body
a rubbish bin
a murderer

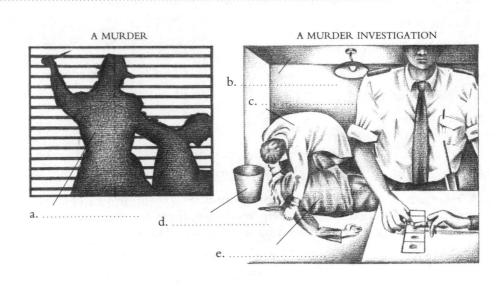

A MURDER   A MURDER INVESTIGATION

b. ....

c. ....

a. ....   d. ....

e. ....

C Read this article about Dr Noguchi.

HE FINDS MURDERERS!

Dr Tom Noguchi, a famous medical examiner in North America, spends a lot of time looking in rubbish bins. He finds things there when he investigates murders. The last thing he does is to go near the body and touch it. Dr Noguchi has a special way of examining a murder.

He never walks in through the front door, but goes in through the back. One of the first places he examines is the kitchen. 'It gives you a person's lifestyle: the kitchen is the centre of activity,' says the doctor. 'Then I go into the bathroom: that is their personal place. They talk to you through their personal things. A body can't say anything, so you have to find something else to talk to you. Then I go to the rubbish bins.'

After he examines the rubbish, he walks up to the body, and stands with his hands pointing at the ceiling. He looks for blood on the ceiling: 'From the blood, you can tell if the killer is left or right handed,' says Dr Noguchi.

D Here is Dr Noguchi's list. This is what he does and looks at when he investigates a murder. Do not re-read the article. Put the actions in the right order. Then re-read the article to check the order.

a. I stand and point at the ceiling. ☐
b. I go into the bathroom. ☐
c. I touch the body. ☐
d. I look in the rubbish bins. ☐

e. I examine the kitchen. ☐
f. I walk up to the body. ☐
g. I look for blood on the ceiling. ☐
h. I enter the house through the back door. ☐

8 International Video Club   reading

Match the descriptions in the video catalogue with the right video.

a
PIERROT LE FOU
A man leaves his wife and runs away with a 17-year-old girl. They travel together to a beautiful island but find only violence.
A classic from the French director Jean-Luc Goddard.

b
SUMMERTIME
A lonely American woman goes on a European vacation, meets an Italian shopkeeper, falls in love, then finds he is married.
Magnificent photography of Venice.

c
THE ADVENTURES OF MARCO POLO
Gary Cooper is the explorer who travels to Peking, visits the emperor and falls in love with a Chinese princess.
Adventure – American style.

d
TAMPOPO
The owner of a restaurant meets a trucker and learns to cook perfect noodles. She also learns some other things ...
A delightful Japanese comedy.

9 Visual dictionary

Complete the visual dictionary for Unit 5 on page 129.

6

THE WAY YOU LOOK

1 Beautiful eyes

A Study these examples. They show the place of adjectives in an English sentence.

Examples: *My <u>young</u> friend has <u>beautiful</u> eyes.*
A <u>happy</u> face is <u>beautiful</u>.
Happiness is a <u>good</u> thing.

Complete the sentences.

1. Adjectives add some information about a .... or pronoun.

   Examples: *a face* (*face* is a noun)
   a happy face (the adjective *happy* adds some information about the face)
   She is happy (*she* is a pronoun; *happy* adds some information about this person).

2. The adjective goes .... the noun, or after the verb *to be*.

B Put these sentences into the right order and underline the adjectives.

1. artistic   usually   is   person   An   lively
2. has   young   an   face   Her   sister   intelligent
3. at   very   is   interviews   smile   A   important
4. mother   a   is   Juanita   proud
5. secretary   ambitious   An   is   serious
6. happy   friend   Our   a   personality   has

2 My bed's too big

too and not enough

A Look at the picture. What's the problem?

Read these sentences.

The bed is too big for the room.
The room is too small.
The room isn't big enough.

B What about your house or flat and the things in it?

Complete the sentences with *too ...* or *not ... enough*.

I think my living room is ....

I think my TV is ....

My car/bicycle is ....

My kitchen is ....

My .... is ....

My ....s are ....

Show your sentences to your teacher, if you like.

3 He is kind, and his kindness is important to me

A Complete the table with nouns or adjectives.

Adjective	Noun	Adjective	Noun
1. kind	....	7.	friendliness
2.	sadness	8. intelligent	....
3. serious	....	9.	confidence
4.	selfishness	10.	beauty
5. lively	....	11. healthy	....
6.	happiness		

B Choose *a* or *b* to complete the sentences.

1. Our boss is popular because she's ....   a. kind   b. kindness
2. Our friend's .... is special.   a. kind   b. kindness
3. Sam is very .... about his work.   a. serious   b. seriousness
4. I'm so happy that my children are ....   a. health   b. healthy
5. Antonia is .... I really like her ....   a. lively   b. liveliness
6. .... people don't always show their ....   a. intelligent   b. intelligence

4 Vowel sounds and sentence rhythms

A ⚏ Listen to the recording. Write down the words you hear in the right column.

1. /æ/ *Words that sound like h<u>a</u>t*   2. /e/ *Words that sound like h<u>ea</u>d*

....

....

....

....

....

B Draw lines to match the two columns. Add *a* or *some* to make sentences like the example.

Example: *I've got a hat for your head.*   *I've got (a or some) ... for your ...*

1. sunglasses	head	....
2. socks	neck	....
3. scarf	feet	....
4. hat	feet	....
5. gloves	eyes	....
6. shoes	hands	....

⚏ Listen and check your answers.

C ⚏ Listen again. What's wrong with the things?

1. The sunglasses are ....   4. The hat is ....
2. The socks are ....   5. The gloves are ....
3. The scarf is ....   6. The shoes are ....

Repeat the dialogues to practise sentence rhythms.

5 Appearance is important

A What is important in appearance? Look at these features. Add at least one new feature. Choose two or three and put them in order of importance for you.

lively eyes   a beautiful body   a happy face   a strong body   a big smile   ....

B 💿 Listen to two people describing their choice. Complete the notes.

Speaker   Important features

1.   *lively* .... ; *nice* , ...
2.   *a big* .... ; *a* .... ; ....

On what feature do the speakers disagree? Are your own choices similar or different?

6 An appearance that shows emotion

A Read the seven sentences. What do you think of them? Do you agree or disagree? What do you think is important in appearance for a fashion photographer?

1. Photographers choose models who are like little girls.
2. Photographers choose models who are a bit similar to them.
3. Photographers photograph their models in situations that are similar to the situations in their own life.
4. Photographers like working with beautiful models – intelligence is not important.
5. Photographers like models with a lot of personality.
6. Photographers are not friends with their models.
7. An appearance that shows emotion is important for photographers.

B Read this article about fashion photographers.

Photographers & MODELS

MANY OF THE world's famous fashion photographers now are women. 'The woman I photograph is definitely a woman, not a little girl,' says Andrea Blanche. 'I guess I choose a woman who is a little bit like me. I get a lot of the situations I photograph my model in from my life. I like working with a woman who is intelligent, lively, and just beautiful to look at. A woman with lots of personality.' Her make-up artist watches the photographer working and says, 'She is friends with her models, they talk a lot, and that is definitely an advantage in the photographs.'

Sheila Metzner, an art director who takes photographs of the country as well as fashion, is a bit different. With a striking face, and a lot of long grey/black hair all around it, she has a mysterious beauty. 'The model I work with has an appearance that speaks, that shows emotion. I like intelligence. But I don't mean just models. I look at women on the street corner, perhaps a woman who is eighty years old. I look for beautiful, strong women. I study them. Photography is a way of studying people.'

But photographers grow old, too. Is it easy to photograph young, beautiful models every morning? 'It's not easy,' Andrea Blanche says. I look in a mirror and I see my face getting older. That's why I work a bit every day on my book.' What book? 'A book about men.'

C Look again at the seven sentences in Part A. What are the answers in the article? Now list the qualities of models that are important for the two photographers.

a. For Andrea Blanche: ....
b. For Sheila Metzner: ....

D Complete the following sentence.

The article says that for women, photographing young models is not always easy because

....

---

7 A job application

reading; listening; writing a job application letter

The Grand Hotel, Inverness
EXPERIENCED RECEPTIONIST REQUIRED.
Shift work. Smart appearance essential.
Must be good with people. Languages an
advantage. Excellent conditions and pay.

A 📼 Listen to Juanita talking about herself. Fill in the missing words in her job application.

Dear Sir,

I would like to apply for the job of hotel receptionist advertised in
the Sunday Herald.

.... twenty-four years old and I think I've got the right
qualifications for the job. I have a certificate from the Cranbury
College of Technology in hotel management. I .... and Spanish
fluently.

I think that I ...... a reasonably .... person and I work hard. My
teachers and friends say that I'm also .... and ....
Working with people is a great pleasure for me. I am single and am
available for night duty.

Thank you for considering my application. I hope to hear from you soon.

Juanita Juarez

B Write a similar letter for yourself. Make any necessary changes. Show your letter to your teacher, if you like.

8 My friend is shy, but very intelligent

Write a few sentences about yourself, your teacher or a friend.

I am (my friend is) … years old. She (he) is …
She (he) has … (what colour hair? what colour eyes? what kind of eyes? face?)
She (he) is … (what kind of personality?)

Next class, show your description to another person or to your teacher, if you like.

9 Visual dictionary

Complete the visual dictionary for Unit 6 on page 130.

10 Reflections

This unit has a lot of words to describe people and their characters.
Try these different ways of remembering words.

1. Make a list of adjectives and colour code them (one colour for positive words and another colour for negative words).
2. Associate each adjective with a person you know.
3. Make a list with a drawing beside each word to remind you of the meaning.

Examples: *happy* *sad* *practical* *artistic*

4. Make a list with a word in your own language that sounds like the word in English.

Example: an English person remembers the Turkish word for February, *şubat*:

February = şubat = shoe.
bat

What works for you? Have you got any other ways?

7

WHAT CAN WE DO?

1 I can't, I really can't

Complete the information.

Positive statement +	Negative statement − (short form)	Negative statement − (long form)	Question
1. I can write.	I can't	I cannot write.	Can I write?
2. You can talk.	You .... talk.	You .... talk.	.... you talk?
3. He can wait.	She	She	.... ?
4. He can play.	....	....	.... ?
5. We can read.	....	....	.... ?
6. They can type.	....	....	.... ?

2 Could you pass the milk, please?

Use *can* or *could* to write the questions for these situations.

Example: You want your brother to pass the milk to you at table.
Could you pass the milk, please? or
Can you pass the milk, please?

1. You want your friend to lend you her book.

   Q: .... ?

2. You ask a friend to get you a cup of tea.

   Q: .... ?

3. You ask your friend to wait a minute –
   you're not quite ready to go.

   Q: .... ?

4. You're at a film with some noisy children.
   You ask them to be quiet and listen.

   Q: .... ?

5. You want your teacher to write a word on the board.

   Q: .... ?

6. You ask an official to show you where to sign a form.

   Q: .... ?

7. You ask a police officer where the bank is.

   Q: .... ?

3 Now and then

present simple; past simple

Birth   5yrs   10   15   20   25   30   35   →

(THEN)   (NOW)

A Which sentences are about THEN? Which sentences are about NOW? Label them *T* or *N*.

1. She was a shy child. □
2. She's a busy parent. □
3. She went to school in her village. □
4. She could play the piano at school. □
5. She hasn't got enough time. □
6. She goes to work at eight in the morning. □
7. Her children go to school on the bus. □

8. She has a lot of friends. □
9. She had a lot of time. □
10. She can't play any musical instrument. □
11. She went home for lunch. □
12. Her children have piano lessons. □
13. She cooks lunch for her children. □
14. She has a sandwich for lunch. □

B What about yourself? Complete these sentences about your life.

When I was a child I was ....

I ....

Now I ....

Show your sentences to your teacher, if you like.

4 I went to school every day

present simple; past simple

Complete the information.

Present (NOW)

1. a. I go to work.
2. a. He/she goes to work.
3. a. They .... to work.

4. a. I am a busy person.
5. a. You .... a busy person.
6. a. She is a busy person.
7. a. We .... busy people.
8. a. They are busy people.

9. a. I have a lot of friends.
10. a. You .... a lot of friends.
11. a. He has a lot of friends.
12. a. We/they .... a lot of friends.

13. a. I can play the piano.
14. a. She .... play the piano.
15. a. We can play the piano.
16. a. They .... play the piano.

Past (THEN)

1. b. I .... to school.
2. b. He/she .... to school.
3. b. They went to school.

4. b. I .... a busy person.
5. b. You were a busy person.
6. b. She .... a busy person.
7. b. We were busy people.
8. b. They .... busy people.

9. b. I had a lot of friends.
10. b. You .... a lot of friends.
11. b. He .... a lot of friends.
12. b. We/they .... a lot of friends.

13. b. I could play the piano.
14. b. She could play the piano.
15. b. We .... play the piano.
16. b. They .... play the piano.

40   Unit 7 WHAT CAN WE DO?

5 I can play the drums   vocabulary

A Complete the sentences using as many different expressions from the box below as possible. Check your answers on page 164.

1. I can use ....
2. I can cook ....
3. I can remember ....
4. I can type ....
5. I can play ....

6. I can write ....
7. I can wash and iron ....
8. I can repair ....
9. I can drive ....
10. I can open ....

> my clothes   the drums   a bank account   a car   a photocopier
> a picture   poems   the guitar   a number   a meal   a computer
> some machines   stories   the piano   a letter   important dates

B Which of the things in Part A can you really do? Tick them, and count your number of ticks. Read what the ticks say about you in the Answer Key.

6 We can play the piano with two fingers!   vocabulary: prepositions

Put in the right word: *at, in, on, with* or *to.*

1. She can read .... her way to work.
2. He can read .... a crowded bus.
3. She reads the newspapers .... the morning.
4. He reads his textbooks .... lunchtime.
5. We can play the piano .... two fingers.
6. They play the piano .... parties.

7. I go .... work, my children go .... school.
8. We go .... a restaurant for lunch.
9. They always go .... the bank at lunchtime.
10. I'm .... work from ten to six.
11. Please write this .... the board.
12. Please write this .... your notebooks.

7 Weak forms   pronunciation

A ☐☐ Listen to the questions and answer them *Yes, I can* or *No, I can't.*

B ☐☐ Now listen to some answers. Pay special attention to the weak forms. Fill in the missing information. Underline the word *can* when it is a weak form.

1. Q: Can you read in a car?

   A: No, I ...., I get sick.

2. Q: Can you type?

   A: ...., ... I can type very quickly, with two fingers.

3. Q: Can you cook a good meal?

   A: ...., ... I can do it in twenty minutes.

4. Q: Can you write a poem?

   A: No, ... I .... think of rhymes.

5. Q: Can you stand on your head?

   A: Yes, of course I can. I .... on my head for five minutes.

6. Q: Can you drive a car?

   A: Well, of course .... I .... even fly a plane.

8 Are you feeling all right, son?

A Read this dialogue between a young boy and his mother. They are Koreans, living in Canada. Can you guess what the missing words are?

1. MOTHER: Hello, son. Good day at ....?

2. SON: Fine, Mum. Can you come here
for a second?

3. MOTHER: Yeah. What's the ....?

4. SON: Isn't life wonderful? I just want
to say that, in spite of everything,
I .... you.

5. MOTHER: Are you feeling all right, son?

6. SON: Very funny, Mum.

7. MOTHER: OK. Let me guess.
How .... do you want?

8. SON: Can you sign my report card?
....

9. MOTHER: How come you have only three As on your report card?

10. SON: No ...., Mum. I .... pass this year easily.

11. MOTHER: Pass? Passing isn't enough! In Korea, students of your age .... all day because they
want to have a good life!

12. SON: But this .... Korea, Mum. Do you want me to study all day?

13. MOTHER: I didn't say that. I want you to study and have good marks. I want you to have a .... life
in the future.

14. SON: A pass is a .... What's the difference? This is the 90s. The world's changed. My friends
have got bad .... too.

15. MOTHER: I don't care about that. I really want to give you a good .... Can't you at least study a bit
more?

B ⬭ Listen to the dialogue and check your guesses. Fill in the missing words.
Underline two examples of *can* used for polite request in this text.

C Can you complete this summary of the dialogue? Add one sentence at the end to
give your own opinion.

1. A young boy shows his report card to ....

2. He wants his mother to sign it. She is not happy about the report card because ....
....

3. The mother wants a lot for her son. She wants him to ....

4. But he is not worried about his report card. He thinks ....

5. I think .... (the mother is right? the son is right? they cannot
understand each other? or ... ?)

A Think of things you can or can't do in the country.

In the country you can .... but you can't

....

Think of things you can or can't do in the city.

In the city you can .... but you can't

....

B Now write a paragraph about yourself.

I prefer to live in .... because …

I can .... and …

In .... I can't …

Show your paragraph to your teacher, if you like.

10 Visual dictionary

Complete the visual dictionary for Unit 7 on page 130.

11 Reflections

What can you do in English? Tick the spaces in the chart.

WHAT CAN YOU DO IN ENGLISH?	I can do this now	I can do this a bit	I can't do this yet
Say hello and goodbye			
Tell someone where a room is in a building			
Describe a room in a house			
Go shopping for food			
Go shopping for clothes			
Ask the price			
Describe a person's appearance			
Describe a person's personality			

What can you do to help with the things you can't do?

– read the units again
– ask for help from the teacher
– talk about it with other students
– spend more time with the Personal Study Workbook and the cassette
– relax and just enjoy learning, even slowly

....

....

8

LOVE IT OR HATE IT!

1 I like sleeping in on Sundays
I like (doing); I usually (do)

Study the examples.

At the weekend, I <u>usually watch</u> television. I **like sleeping in**, but I <u>don't usually</u> because I have too much work.
On Saturdays, my father <u>does</u> the shopping. He **doesn't like doing it**, but he <u>always does</u> it.

> **HELP**
> sleep in = sleep late

Write three sentences about what you usually do at the weekend, and what you like doing at the weekend.

Show your sentences to your teacher, if you like.

2 Pollution is a problem in our city
vocabulary

A Check these words and put them under one of the two headings. Use a dictionary if you need to.

Facilities

....
....
....
....
....
....

Possible problems

....
....
....
....
....
....

pollution	shops	noise	traffic	parks	cinemas	crowds	prices
markets	restaurants	bridges					

B Look through the unit and add more words.

44   <u>Unit 8 LOVE IT OR HATE IT!</u>

3 How many legs have spiders got?

A Look at these animals and insects. Add the missing names. Put the names into the right columns.

fly   mosquito   spider   snake   cockroach   cat   dog

1. They've got tails	2. They've got four legs	3. They've got six legs
....	....	....
....	....	....
....	....	....
....	....	....
....	....	

B 🎧 Listen to the questions. Answer them. (Be honest!)

Example: (Question on the recording) *Do you like cats?*
You answer: *Yes* or *Yes, I do* or *No, I don't* or *No, I hate them.*

4 The vowel sounds in *dog* and *goat*

A Can you guess the missing words?

1. The frog's on the ....

2. The dog's in the ....

3. The goat's in the ....

4. The hippo's at the ....

5. The mosquito's on my ....

6. Show me the way to go ....

B 🎧 Listen and fill in the missing words.
Underline the sounds that are like d<u>o</u>g /ɒ/.
Circle the sounds that are like g<u>oa</u>t /əʊ/.

5 Rhythm rap with 'h'

A 🎧 Listen and join in with: *She's happy, and he's happy too.*

He's artistic and she's athletic,
Her hair's red and his hair's white, BUT
She's happy, and he's happy too.

He's in Hamburg and she's in Holland,
He's in a hotel and she's at home, BUT
She's happy, and he's happy too.

She hates shopping and he hates driving,
She loves dogs and he loves hippos, BUT
She's happy, and he's happy too.

B Now say the other lines too. You can hear the first line of each verse and the line:
She's happy, and he's happy too on the recording.

A 💿 Listen and complete the sentences.

1. *Speaker 1*

   At the weekends he likes .... because he .... so hard during the
   week. And on Sunday he .... roller skating, ...

2. *Speaker 2*

   At the weekends, she usually .... the children swimming in the morning and then
   they .... and they go to the .... in the afternoon.

3. *Speaker 3*

   On Saturdays he .... wakes up quite early. Then he usually .... and
   .... the papers and .... breakfast.

4. *Speaker 4*

   On Saturdays she normally .... her shopping, which is something she doesn't really
   .... doing. And then in the afternoon she .... her child to the park. On
   Sunday she .... a nice long breakfast and .... the newspaper.

B 💿 Now listen and complete the information about what the next four speakers
don't like or hate.

1. She hates .... and sitting on a .... behind a long row of traffic.

2. He hates .... in traffic, in a long queue. And he also hates .... the
   ....

3. She hates ....

4. He doesn't mind ...., but he hates ....

Expatriates are people who go to live in another country for a few years or more, often with
their families. Sometimes they work for an international company. Successful expatriates are
people who can live happily in a new country.

A Complete the sentences in column 1 to show your opinion.

Column 1	*Column 2*
I think that *successful expatriates ...*	*The text says that* *successful expatriates ...*
are	are ....
like	like ....
love	love ....

B On the next page, there is a text about 'successful expatriate wives' – women who
go with their husbands to a new country and are happy there. Read the text and
complete the sentences in column 2. Are your ideas similar to those in the text?

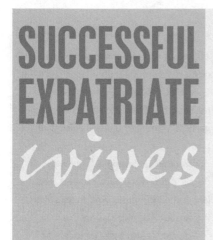

SUCCESSFUL EXPATRIATE *wives*

People say that successful expatriates are those who get a lot of pleasure from living in a different culture. They love travel for itself; they are curious, they love new experiences; they love trying new and exotic foods; they like meeting new people; they read a lot about the country; they are adventurous and they have a direct interest in the new culture. These people generally have a cheerful and positive nature; they are enthusiastic and they seem to be exceptionally healthy.

Successful expatriate wives love travelling. They have a long history of travelling, even before their husband's job in the new country. One of these successful wives said: 'I just love people. I travel all the time; I went to Sweden when I was only five years old. This increased my interest in travelling. Now I just want to go on travelling.'

This type of wife makes a successful expatriate wife. She gives her family the idea that living in a new culture is a joy. She supports her husband in his work and she helps her family to settle in easily. This type of wife often turns out to be a happy 'cosmopolitan' – someone who is at home in all parts of the world.

---

8 Yes, I love travelling
listening

A 📟 Listen to two interviews with people from other countries now living in England. Gertrude is a German woman and Jean-Pierre comes from France. Complete the information in the table.

	Gertrude	Jean-Pierre
1. Do they like living in England?	*Yes*	
2. What do they like about living in a different culture?		*the difference at all levels*
3. Are they cheerful?	*I think so*	
4. Do they love travel?		
5. Do they love trying new foods?		*Yes*
6. Do they read about the new country?		

B Write answers to these questions.

1. What qualities make Gertrude and Jean-Pierre successful expatriates?

....

2. They are different in one way from the 'successful expatriates' described in the article. What is that difference?

....

---

9 Welcome to South Australia
reading

A What is popular with tourists? Make sure you understand the words in this list. Which of them do you think are important for tourists?

beaches	shopping	restaurants	parks	discos	pubs	bars
a casino	museums	art galleries				

B Read this tourist brochure about Adelaide, in South Australia.

WELCOME TO SOUTH AUSTRALIA
and enjoy your holiday!

Adelaide

SOUTH AUSTRALIA HAS wonderful sights, sounds and tastes! Adelaide, the capital city, is full of colour. There are over 30 kilometres of sparkling white beaches for you.

Shopping is an excellent activity for all visitors to Adelaide. The city has some very interesting stores. Rundle Mall in the centre of the city is a major shopping centre. Normal shopping hours are Mon–Thurs 9 am to 5.30 pm, Saturday 9 am to 5 pm and Friday nights until 9 pm.

Adelaide has got hundreds of restaurants, from cheap bistros to formal restaurants, and Adelaide's Mediterranean climate is perfect for eating out of doors in the pavement cafés.

Adelaide is fun to explore. There are many parks around the city centre, and gardens with many unusual Australian plants.

After dark, Adelaide is lively with discos, pubs, piano bars, cabarets, rock, jazz and dance music. And there's also the famous Adelaide Casino!

Adelaide is also a city for lovers of history – it's got many excellent museums, including the South Australian Museum and the Art Gallery of South Australia, both on North Terrace.

Welcome to South Australia and enjoy your holiday!

What has Adelaide got for tourists? Make a list.

10 A tourist brochure for our town
writing

Prepare a tourist brochure for your town. Write a paragraph, like this:

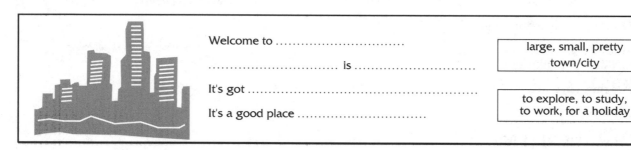

Welcome to ....

.... is ....

It's got ....

It's a good place ....

large, small, pretty town/city

to explore, to study, to work, for a holiday

Show your paragraph to your teacher, if you like.

11 Visual dictionary

Complete the visual dictionary for Unit 8 on page 131.

12 Reflections

Make notes about your learning. Put the phrases in the box under the appropriate heading. Add others.

I like	I quite like	I don't like
....	....	....
....	....	....
....	....	....
....	....	....

reading English
speaking English
listening to English
studying English
grammar
learning new words
learning alone
meeting other learners

9

THOSE WERE THE DAYS

1 Was your life happy?

past tense question forms

A Imagine your grandmother is in the room with you now. You want to ask her some questions about the past. Add the verbs to the questions.

1. Where .... you born?
2. When .... you born?
3. .... your life happy?
4. What .... the names of your children?
5. .... your children good?
6. .... your life very hard?
7. .... your house comfortable?
8. What .... your favourite room?
9. .... the shops close to your house?
10. .... your town very crowded?

11. .... music an important part of your life?
12. .... the winters very cold?
13. Where .... you live when you were a child?
14. .... you go to school?
15. .... you move a lot when you were a child?
16. .... you ever live in a different country?
17. .... you live in the country, or in a city?
18. When .... you get married?
19. How many times .... you .... married?
20. How many children .... you have?

Check your answers on page 165. Then do Part B.

B A grandfather answered some questions. Here are his answers. Write the questions.

1. Q: ....? A: I was born in 1901.
2. Q: ....? A: When I was a child, we lived in the country.
3. Q: ....? A: I went to the school in my village.
4. Q: ....? A: I got married in 1920.
5. Q: ....? A: Yes, my life was happy, because I had a very good wife.
6. Q: ....? A: I had six children.

2 I phoned them from home

simple past; object pronouns

A There are five mistakes (with object pronouns) in these sentences.

Example: *He lived with his mother. He liked living with him.*
    Correct sentence: *He liked living with <u>her</u>.*

Find the mistakes and correct them.

Barry lived in New Zealand with his mother. He lived with them until 1985, when he got married. At first he stayed in the same town with his wife and mother, but later he moved with him to New York. He loved the big city so much that he mentioned them in one of his newspaper articles. But he missed his friend Tom. He wanted Tom to come to New York too. So one day he telephoned Tom and asked her to take the next plane to New York. He was surprised when Tom refused. But then his friend announced that he too had got married. He now had a lovely wife and two daughters, and he wanted to stay in New Zealand with it.

B Complete the answers.

1. Q: When did you phone your mother?   A: I phoned .... at three.

2. Q: Where did you see your brother?   A: I saw .... at the cinema.

3. Q: What did you buy for your sister?   A: I got .... a new scarf.

4. Q: How much did you pay for the scarf?   A: I paid a lot for ....

5. Q: Did you remember to phone your parents?   A: Yes, I phoned .... from home.

3 My life story
practice with past tenses

Read Livia's life story. Fill in the blanks with the correct form of the verb.

1. I .... (to be) born in England, but my parents .... (to be) not English. My father .... (to be) from Poland, and my mother .... (to be) Russian. I .... (to go) to school in Bournemouth, where my father .... (to be) a dentist. When I .... (to finish) school, I .... (to decide) to travel.

2. I .... (to go) to Russia to see my grandmother. But on the way I .... (to visit) Rome, and there I .... (to go) to a dentist. He was wonderful! Like my father! I .... (to get married) and .... (to stay) in Italy. I .... (to have) two children.

3. Then we .... (to move) to Bucharest. When we .... (to arrive), I didn't know anybody. I .... (to be) lonely. So I .... (to decide) to be a teacher. I .... (to be) very good at English, of course, so I .... (to start) to teach English. Now we live in Germany. I still teach English, but now I teach at the university.

4 I started a new job yesterday
reading; pronunciation

A Read this story and put the pictures in the right order. Number them from 1 to 6. Find eighteen verbs in the simple past tense and underline them.

I started a new job yesterday.
They asked me to work late on my first day.
I stayed until eight o'clock.
They wanted me to stay until nine.
I refused.
So they sacked me.
I tried to explain my reasons, but
they phoned for a taxi.
I walked out crying.
They laughed at me.
I hated every minute of that job.
The taxi driver played some nice music,
and when we arrived at my home,
I thanked him.
He called out: 'You looked sad, it seemed a pity.'
I smiled ... just another day!

B 📼 Listen to the story. Write each verb in one of these lists, if it has the same sound at the end of the word. Listen to the examples first.

/t/ (t)	/ɪd/ (ed)	/d/ (d)
1. They sack**ed** me	2. I hat**ed** every minute	3. He call**ed** out
....	....	....
....	....	....
....	....	....
....	....	....

5 Did you use the phone yesterday?   listening

📼 Listen to the questions.
Answer them truthfully. Say either:

Yes, I / you / she / he / it / we / they did.   *or*   No, I / you / she / he / it / we / they didn't.

6 The shark   reading

A Match the nine expressions with a definition.

1. a shark
2. bait for the fishing line
3. a wool broker
4. to borrow money
5. to form a business partnership
6. to be at war with
7. to announce
8. to buy the entire wool crop
9. to earn a fortune

a. to get a lot of money
b. to fight another country
c. a very big fish that can eat people
d. someone who buys wool and then sells it again
e. to get money from someone for a time, then pay it back
f. the small fish that is put on a fishing line to catch bigger fish
g. to start a business with someone
h. to say
i. to buy all the wool that a country produces

B Read the story.

A hungry young man with no money walked along Sydney harbour shore past a shark fisherman. The fisherman asked him to take a turn with his fishing line to bring him good luck. Immediately, the young man managed to get a shark, 5.8 metres long. The fisherman opened up the fish and walked off to get some more bait for his fishing line. When he returned, the young man walked away.

The young man walked into a hotel to have breakfast, then he went into the offices of a very rich wool broker. He asked to see the owner. He announced that he wanted to borrow 100,000 pounds. The broker was surprised, but he decided to listen. The young man insisted that they form a business partnership and buy the entire wool crop, worth 2.5 million pounds. The broker asked for the reason. The man answered: 'Because France is at war with Germany, and the price of wool is up 14 per cent in London.'

The wool broker produced the latest London paper from a boat that arrived the previous night, 50 days out of London (the overland telegraph was still not finished). The paper mentioned nothing of war or high wool prices. The young man then surprised him by producing a copy of a London newspaper only ten days old and the pocket diary of a German sailor. Both were from the shark's stomach.

The wool broker was both surprised and very happy. Together the two men formed a partnership and the young man earned his first fortune.

C Choose the right answer. Tick the boxes.

1. The fisherman asked the young man to
   a. give him some bait for his line ☐   b. try to get a shark ☐   c. buy some wool ☐
2. The young man immediately managed to
   a. get a big shark ☐   b. get some bait ☐   c. open the fish ☐
3. The young man asked the wool broker for
   a. a newspaper ☐   b. some money ☐   c. a boat ☐
4. The wool broker had a newspaper that was
   a. 10 days old ☐   b. one month old ☐   c. 50 days old ☐
5. The young man showed the broker
   a. a newspaper from the shark's stomach ☐   b. the entire wool crop ☐   c. a business partnership ☐
6. The young man wanted to buy wool because the price of wool
   a. was not high ☐   b. was too high ☐   c. was going up because of the war ☐
7. The young man and the broker
   a. talked but did nothing ☐   b. got very rich ☐   c. had breakfast together ☐

D Why is this story probably not true? Can you think of two reasons?

It probably isn't true because ....

It probably isn't true because ....

🔲 Listen to two people giving their reasons. What are their reasons?

1. There are .... in the sea near .... or Germany.

2. A shark .... to reach Sydney in ten days.

3. In a shark's stomach, a newspaper ....

4. A fisherman is .... by hand.

Are their reasons similar to yours?

---

7 Little arguments   listening; writing

A Study this little argument.

A: You were late.
B: No, I wasn't. I was here on time.
A: No, you weren't, you were late.
B: I wasn't.
A: You were, I looked at my watch.

B Now write three little arguments. The first lines are there for you.

1. C: It was October the 3rd.

   D: No, it wasn't, it was ....

   C: ....

   D: ....

2. E: She was a great boss.

   F: You're crazy, she ....

   E: ....

   F: ....

3. G: They were yellow.

   H: ....

   G: ....

   H: ....

52

C ▭ Now listen to three little arguments. Fill in the words. Are they similar to yours?

1. C: It was October the 3rd.

   D: No, no it wasn't, it was ....

   C: ....

   D: ....

   C: ....

   D: ....

   C: ....

2. E: She was a great boss.

   F: Are you crazy? She ....

   E: ....

   F: ....

   E: ....

3. G: They were yellow.

   H: ....

   G: ....

   H: ....

   G: ....

   H: ....

8 Visual dictionary

Complete the visual dictionary for Unit 9 on page 132.

9 Reflections

Did you study a language at school? Are there any differences?

At school, I studied …
It was (easy? hard? interesting? or … ?)
Now, learning English is different, because we (listen to a lot of things? talk a lot? because there are many different things to do in the books? or … ?)

....

....

....

....

....

10

ONCE UPON A TIME

---

1 I didn't go to work last week because I was ill positive, negative, and question forms

A Answer the following questions. Show your answers to your teacher, if you like.

Example: Q: *Did you have an English class last week?*
 A: *Yes, in fact I had two English classes last week.*
 or *No, we didn't have an English class, because our teacher was ill.*

1. Q: Did you meet your friends last week? A: ....

2. Q: Did you go to the cinema last week? A: ....

3. Q: Did you find or lose anything last week? A: ....

4. Q: Did you buy anything interesting last week? A: ....

5. Q: What did you do on Sunday last week? A: ....

B Here are some answers about last week. Write the questions.

1. Q: .... ?
 A: Yes, I'm very sorry, I forgot about our meeting.

2. Q: .... ?
 A: Yes, I went to the cinema with two of my friends.

3. Q: .... ?
 A: We saw an old film: *Jurassic Park*.

4. Q: .... ?
 A: No, I didn't speak to the manager; I spoke to the secretary instead.

5. Q: .... ?
 A: She told me to come back next week.

---

2 She caught a train to Valencia vocabulary

A Put the verbs into the past tense.
Then put them into the diagram.

Example: *to hear – I heard*

to hear	to catch
to eat	to see
to go	to come
to run	to write
to say	to speak
to tell	to read

with my ears
.... *I heard* ....

with my feet
....
....
....

I did this

with my hands
....
....

with my eyes
....
....

with my mouth
....
....
....
....

B How many words in the box below go with these verbs?

Example: *You wrote … a book, some music, a newspaper*

1. He heard ....

2. She caught ....

3. We ate ....

4. They saw ....

5. I read ....

a book	a train	a meal
a sound	a painting	
a ball	some music	
an apple	a small child	
a scream	a newspaper	
a little cottage	a shot	
a light	a fish	

---

3 Last week I went to the theatre   vocabulary; writing

How many sentences can you write about what happened to you last week?

📼 Listen to someone talking about what happened last week. Complete these sentences.

1. On Saturday she .... and they ....

2. They saw a ....

3. At the end, they .... and .... , but she ....

   ....

4. They were hungry, so they .... and ....

5. They had .... and ....

6. Suddenly, it ....

7. She ....

8. Luckily, the theatre .... But she was soaking wet!

Are any of your sentences like the ones on the tape?

---

4 Rhythm rap   pronunciation

A Here is a story about a fisherman. Fill in the blanks, using the words in the box.

The fisherman comes home

And did you catch a fish, son?   I .... a lot.

And did you buy a lemon?   Oh, I ....

And did you clean the fish, then?   It .... too hot.

Well, did you have a nice day?   Oh, I just ....

And did you bring the fish home?   Er … I .... the cat.

And what about our meal then?   Can't you .... that?

I'll show you what I CAN do!   'My head!' he said.

forgot	sat	was	do	fed	caught

B 📼 Listen and check your answers.

**Now listen again. You play the part of the
fisherman and give his replies.**

A Here are two stories from different parts of the world.

1. Find the pictures that go with each story and put them in the right order.

2. The verbs in brackets are in the present tense. Put them into the past tense.

a ☐   b ☐   c ☐   d ☐

e ☐   f ☐   g ☐

1 *'The first sunrise', a legend from Australia*

Once, long ago, the sky .... (is) very close to the earth, and people .... (walk) on their hands and knees. They .... (can) not stand up. The magpies .... (are) intelligent birds. They .... (think) they .... (can) raise the sky. They .... (get) sticks and .... (push). They raised the sky a little bit, and then they .... (get) big stones and rested the sky on them. People stood up. The birds .... (raise) the sky again. Suddenly it split open, and people .... (see) the first beautiful sunrise. The magpies started singing. After that, the birds always sang at sunrise.

2 *'How the birds made the world', from the Pacific Coast of Canada*

Once upon a time the world .... (is) shut up inside a big shell, like an oyster. The birds flew over the big shell. They .... (see) that the world .... (is) closed, they .... (hear) the people inside shouting. They .... (get) large stones and .... (drop) them on the shell. The shell .... (opens) up a little bit. The birds .... (catch) the edge of the shell with their beaks and .... (pull). The shell split open and people .... (run) out into the sunlight. The birds .... (fly) away and .... (leave) the people in their new world.

CD Listen to the stories and check your answers.

B True or false? Write *T* or *F* in the boxes.

1. The two stories are about how the world began. ☐

Story 1
2. The birds walked on their hands and knees. ☐
3. The people could not at first stand up and see the sun. ☐
4. The people raised the sky. ☐
5. Story 1 explains why birds sing at sunrise. ☐

Story 2
6. The birds were singing inside a big shell. ☐
7. The birds dropped stones onto the shell. ☐
8. The birds caught the edge of the shell and closed it. ☐
9. When the shell opened, the people stayed inside. ☐

Did you like the stories? Do you have stories in your country about how the world began?

A Match the pictures
and the words.
Put the right letters
in the boxes.

1. a fossil ☐
2. a dinosaur ☐
3. a plant ☐
4. a lizard ☐
5. a horn ☐
6. a zoo ☐
7. a scientist ☐

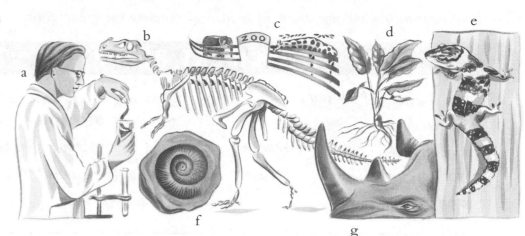

B Read this newspaper article about fossils.

At the beginning of the nineteenth century, the study of fossils began. Before it began, people did not believe that fossils once lived.

The most famous fossils of all are the dinosaurs. Now, of course, there are no dinosaurs. They all died millions of years before people lived in the world. Scientists still do not know why the dinosaurs died.

Many scientists believe that dinosaurs died after a change of climate. The earth got cold, and many plants and animals died.

The British scientist Richard Owen invented the word *dinosaur* 150 years ago. He used two Greek words, *deinos* and *sauros*, meaning terrible lizards. Some dinosaurs could run rapidly on two legs. Others had horns to protect them. Some dinosaurs ate plants, for example triceratops and stegosaurus. Others ate meat, like the giant tyrannosaurus, which stood up to seven metres high.

C Here are answers to ten questions about the article. Complete the questions.

1. Q: When .... the study of fossils ....?

   A: It began in the nineteenth century.

2. Q: Why are there ....?

   A: Because they all died.

3. Q: Why .... all the dinosaurs ....?

   A: Scientists don't know. Maybe the earth got cold, and plants and animals died.

4. Q: Who .... the word ....?

   A: The British scientist Richard Owen.

5. Q: When .... Richard Owen .... the word *dinosaur*?

   A: 150 years ago.

6. Q: Could ....?

   A: Yes, some dinosaurs could run rapidly on two legs.

7. Q: What .... some dinosaurs have ....?

   A: They had horns to protect them.

8. Q: What ....?

   A: Some dinosaurs ate plants, and some ate animals.

⫘ Listen to the questions and check your answers.

🎧 Listen to someone talking about an accident. Complete the report form.

)) ACCIDENT REPORT ((

1. Date of accident: *Monday,* ....

2. Time of accident: *10 am* ....

3. Place of accident: *Near the market, on the corner of   Street and Main Street.*

4. Description of the accident: *A car went round the corner and straight into a   stand. The stand shattered and the car hit Ms. F. Alonzo and knocked her   .*

---

8 Visual dictionary

Complete the visual dictionary for Unit 10 on page 133.

9 Reflections

Irregular verbs are difficult to remember. Do these ways help you?

1. Make a list of verbs that have the same sound in the past.

Example: *sing/sang* and *ring/rang*
          bring/brought and *catch/caught*

2. Make a list of important verbs. Use different colours to write in the present tense and the past tense.

Example: *I go to work* (blue)   *Yesterday, I went to work* (red)
          He says nothing (blue)   *Yesterday, he said nothing* (red)

3. Write sentences about your life, using as many verbs as you can. Underline the verbs.

Example: *I was born in Mexico. I came to the US when I was nine. I never forgot my home town.*

4. List verbs in categories. Try this way now:

Here are some categories. Add verbs to each category. Add one or more categories.

Some verbs change to *ang*:   ....

Some verbs change to *aught*:   ....

Some verbs change to *an*:   ....

Some verbs change to *oke*:   ....

Some verbs change to *ote*:   ....

Some verbs change to *ame*:   *to come - he came*

Some verbs ....:   ....

........................:   ....

5. Do you know of any other ways? ....

11

WHAT'S GOING ON?

1 At the moment I'm studying English
present simple; present continuous

Here is a list of verbs.

read	write	watch	play	eat	drink	wash	live	study
get	find	draw	drive	walk	run	go shopping	learn	
build	have	answer	listen to	fly to	make			

Choose six verbs. Use the verbs to write three sentences about yourself, your family or friends. Study the example first.

Example: *I usually* <u>play</u> *football, but today I can't, because I'm* <u>studying</u> *for an exam.*

1. I usually .... , but at the moment ....
   ....

2. I (or someone you know) usually .... , but just now ....
   ....

3. Normally, I (or someone you know) .... , but today ....
   ....

Show your sentences to your teacher, if you like.

2 What are you doing? I'm studying English
long/short forms; questions and negatives

A Complete the information about question forms.

Long	*Short*
1. Am I learning?	*no short form*
2. Are you/they learning?	*no short form*
3. Is he/she learning?	*no short form*
4. What am I learning?	*no short form*
5. What are you learning?	What're you learning? (spoken form)
6. What is he learning?	What's he ....?
7. What ...... she learning?	.... she ....?
8. .... are they learning?	....? (spoken form)

B Complete the questions and answers.

1. Q: What .... doing?   A: I'm reading a book.
2. Q: Why .... you .... that book?   A: It's interesting.
3. Q: What .... your sister doing?   A: ....'s building a chair.
4. Q: What's your friend doing?   A: She's .... television.
5. Q: What .... your friends doing?   A: ....'re .... to the cinema.
6. Q: What .... we doing now?   A: We .... learning English.

C **Write the present continuous form for the underlined verbs.**

1. I usually <u>have</u> tea at four.   I'm .... tea early today.

2. You usually <u>listen</u> to music.   Today, you're .... to the news.

3. He usually <u>makes</u> a cake.   Today, he's .... a meal.

4. She usually <u>writes</u> a letter.   Today, she's .... an article.

5. We usually <u>live</u> in Portugal.   This year, we're .... in France.

6. They usually <u>get</u> bread.   Today, they're .... cake.

7. They usually <u>run</u> for the bus.   Today, they're .... for the train.

Here are two pictures of beach scenes from different centuries. Complete the two descriptions.

In painting a, there is a group of people on a beach. They are camping. A fire ....

.... There are some fish nearby. Two people are .... in

a little hut made from some trees. Three men are .... One man is

.... A young boy ....

There are also two dogs. They're ....

In painting b, there are many people on a beach. There is a bridge with several people on it.

A man, a woman and a girl .... Another woman ....

.... In front of the bridge, there are three people. One woman is ....

.... One man

.... Another man ....

.... Behind the bridge, an older man ....

.... Further away,

behind the bridge, many people ....

Which words from the box go with these sentence beginnings?

1. I'm having ....

2. She's building ....

3. He's listening to ....

4. They're learning ....

5. We're watching ....

6. You're reading ....

7. I'm making ....

8. They're flying to ....

9. She's answering ....

10. He's calling ....

the news	the telephone
a book	the radio
Spain a cake	a table
a film Tokyo	
a cup of tea	a new house
a party a meal	
a shower	television
English	the doorbell
me football	
the present continuous tense	
music his friend	
to cook	a question
a new language	a taxi

A ▭ Listen to a reporter from the past giving a news flash about a historic event. Match each report with one of the titles below.

a **Strange White Men Appear on the Shore**

b **The President Murdered**

c **Lava is Pouring over Pompeii**

B Now complete the details about the event.

Lava is Pouring over Pompeii

The reporter is standing in the central square. There is .... everywhere.

Lava .... to pour down the mountain. People ....

everything they can and .... the city. The roads are full of people ....

get away.

The President Murdered

The whole city .... for the President's car. There are many people ....

by the side of the road, some waving flags. The President .... in the back seat

beside the First Lady. They're both .... and .... to the crowds. There is a

shot. The President is slumping forwards.

Strange White Men Appear on the Shore

The reporter is on the beach. There is a big white monster on the water. A boat ......

.... the monster and is coming over the water. Many people .... on

the beach. Some .... their hands and some .... Strange

people are in the boat. They .... wearing very strange-coloured clothes and their skin is

very .... And now, they're .... of the boat, and coming onto the

beach. The people .... back in fear ...

A Do you know these expressions? Match them with a definition and then check your answers on page 167.

1. to complain
2. to read for pleasure
3. a novel
4. rubbish
5. to some extent
6. to grow out of something

a. a bit, not completely
b. a long book with a story in it
c. something that is not good, terrible, not useful
d. to become too old for something
e. to read because you want to and you like it
f. to say you don't like something

B Do you agree with the following statements completely, or a bit? Tick the appropriate column.

	I agree completely	*I agree a bit*	*I don't agree*	*I don't know*
All teenagers do is watch television, listen to terrible pop music and complain about school.	☐	☐	☐	☐
Teenagers don't read any more.	☐	☐	☐	☐
Teenagers only read rubbish.	☐	☐	☐	☐
Teenagers spend a lot of money on magazines.	☐	☐	☐	☐
Teenagers like long novels.	☐	☐	☐	☐
Teenagers like to read about health, the environment and popular science.	☐	☐	☐	☐

C Now read this article. It is about what teenagers are reading in Great Britain.

teenagers reading?

»»»what are

Are teenagers reading anything at all any more? Or are they – as parents and teachers think – simply spending all their time listening to music and watching television? We interviewed parents and teenagers to find out. Here are the results of our questionnaire.

PARENTS SAY: All teenagers do is watch television, listen to terrible pop music and complain about school.

Well, parents are right to some extent. Our questionnaire shows that teenagers are spending on average 80% of their free time listening to music or watching television. **BUT** the questionnaire also shows that 72% of teenagers are reading for pleasure every week.

PARENTS SAY: Teenagers don't read any more!

Again, parents are right to some extent. Children don't buy many books after they reach the age of 11. After that, children spend a lot on videos, cassettes and posters. They don't spend very much on books.
BUT the questionnaire shows that teenagers are reading a lot of magazines! In fact, 40% of children from 13 to 19 spend money on comics and magazines.

PARENTS SAY: Teenagers only read rubbish!

Parents are probably not completely right. According to our questionnaire, teenagers are buying a variety of magazines, many of them about health and fitness, the environment and popular science. They are also becoming more critical of comics and teen magazines. They feel they are growing out of this kind of reading.
BUT they say that they don't have time to read long novels. They can't get interested in them. And yes, they prefer videos, films and going out!

D Here is what parents and teachers think about teenagers in Great Britain. Are they right? Complete the summary.

1. *Parents and teachers think that teenagers watch television, listen to music and complain about school.*

   The questionnaire shows that teenagers are spending 80% of their free time ....

   or .... But 72% of teenagers ....

2. *Parents and teachers think that teenagers don't read any more.*

   The questionnaire shows that children are not .... books after the age of

   ...., but they are ....

3. *Parents and teachers think that teenagers only read rubbish.*

   The questionnaire shows that teenagers are ....

4. But teenagers aren't reading long novels. They prefer ....

7 A DIY card   writing

Are some of your family or friends too busy to write to you? Complete the following DIY (Do It Yourself) card to send to them. Fill in the blank spaces with an appropriate expression.

Dear	☐ Mum	☐ Dad	☐ Friend	☐ ....

You are not answering my letters. I guess you haven't got time. This is a card to help you. Just tick the appropriate boxes and send it back to me.

I am feeling	☐ very well	☐ quite well	☐	☐ very sick
I am	☐ working very hard	☐		☐ not doing anything at the moment
I am	☐ enjoying life enormously	☐ having a		☐ feeling very depressed
I am	☐	☐		☐ ....
I hope you are	☐ very well and happy	☐		☐ ....
☐ Lots of love	☐ Best wishes	☐		☐ ....

8 Visual dictionary

Complete the visual dictionary for Unit 11 on page 134.

9 Reflections

Complete these sentences.

My thoughts about learning English:

I'm enjoying ....

I'm not enjoying ....

I'm finding it hard to ....

I'm finding it easy to ....

12

MAKING PLANS

Complete the sentences about the seven people. Number 1 is an example.

1. Now she's ..*typing*...... a letter, but after work she's ..*meeting*..... a friend.

2. Now .... bringing two cups of coffee, but after work .... the cinema.

3. At the moment she's .... notes, but after work ....'s having a guitar lesson.

4. Now she's .... a client, but after work she's .... to Bangkok.

5. Now .... discussing computers, but after work they're .... a meal together at the ....

6. At the moment ...., but .... football.

7. At the moment she's .... a memo, but ....

2 We're going to the restaurant on Monday evening

the future; time expressions

A Study the examples.

Examples:
I'm going to the beach <u>this weekend</u>.
We're going to the restaurant <u>on Monday evening</u>.
He's going to the shops <u>on Saturday</u>.
She's going to Africa <u>in January</u>.

We're going to the seaside <u>in the summer</u>.
We're meeting outside the cinema <u>at eight o'clock</u>.
They're coming to dinner <u>tonight</u>.

B Each sentence has one mistake. Rewrite the sentences so that they are correct.

1. We're going shopping at Friday.

....

2. Are you going to your English class this tonight?

....

3. The manager flying to Belgium in December.

....

4. Don't forget: the meeting is on 9 o'clock.

....

5. We always take our holidays at the winter.

....

6. Are you visiting a friend in this weekend?

....

7. They not playing tennis on Saturday afternoon.

....

8. We're meeting them at 3 o'clock at Monday morning.

....

3 We're going on holiday!

vocabulary

Put the expressions from the box into the right place. Read Unit 12 in the Class Book and try to add other words to the diagram.

bus	my family
party	play football
cinema	shops
work	school
drive	the children
picnic	holiday
boat	market
play tennis	bed

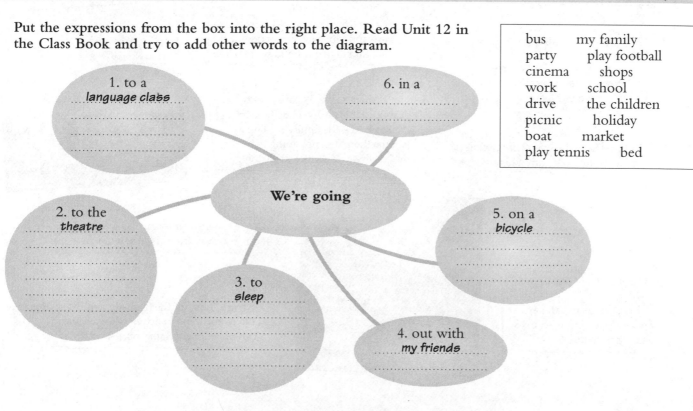

4 -ing sounds and sentence rhythm

A Read these questions and answers. Can you fill in the blanks? The missing words rhyme with the last word in the line.

1. Q: What are you doing this weekend, Alex?   A: I'm making a ...., and I'm going to the lake.

2. Q: What are you doing this weekend, Pat?   A: I'm reading a ...., and I'm learning to cook.

3. Q: What are you doing this weekend, Olivia?   A: I'm buying a ...., and I'm getting a cat.

4. Q: What are you doing this weekend, Tony?   A: I'm going to the ...., and I'm buying a peach.

5. Q: What are you doing this weekend, you two?   A: I'm playing a ...., and she's doing the same.

▱▱ Listen and check your answers.

B ▱▱ Listen again. This time, you answer the questions.

5 Where are you going on holiday?

A A newspaper asked five English people about their holiday plans. Read the beginning of their answers. Guess how each one continues. Match the endings with the beginnings.

1   Peter Middleton, Chief Executive, Thomas Cook:
I'm going to Indonesia for ten days.

2   Mike Smith, doctor:
My wife and I are going to Corsica.

3   Anne Winterton, MP:
We're going to Portugal for two or three weeks in September.

4   Eamonn Fahey, egg deliverer, theatre worker:
I'm going to Malta for two weeks with my girfriend because I've got an apartment there.

5   Cliff Michelmore, travel broadcaster:
I'm not going to go anywhere.

6   Caroline Dawney, literary agent:
This year, as usual, I am going bicycling with my son in Somerset.

a   We're going to lie on the beach and go to discos and relax. Why do we go there? There aren't many places left where the English are really liked.

b   I go on holiday to get my son, who's 11, away from his computer. We're going to stay at lovely bed and breakfast places and we're going to enjoy meeting new dogs.

c   I come from the Isle of Wight. I live here and I love it. We spend our time here and take our holidays here too.

d   I lived there for two years twenty years ago. It's partly a business tour of the Far East – the family's going to join me there. I'm not going to lie on the beach – I don't like sunbathing.

e   We go there every year. It's informal and we can get away from the pressures of work.

f   We are going for the fresh air, and the sailing. We're not going to lie on the beach and it's certainly not good for you, especially at my age.

B 📼 Listen and check your answers.

C Answer these questions about the people who talked about their holiday plans.

1. Who is going to stay at home? ....
2. Who is going to go to a country in Asia? ....
3. Who is going to go on a boat? ....
4. Who is going to go to a place where English people are popular? ....
5. Who is going to go back to a place where he lived long ago? ....
6. Who is going to spend some time cycling? ....
7. Who is going to get away from work and be informal? ....
8. Who is going to spend time on the beach and in discos? ....

6 I'm going to the beach ...   writing

Where are you going on your next holiday? Write a short paragraph about it.

7 Visual dictionary

Complete the visual dictionary for Unit 12 on page 135.

8 Reflections

MON	FRI
TUES ● FULL MOON	SAT
WED	SUN
THURS	NOTES

What are you going to do this week to help your English? Write notes in the diary.

13

BETTER AND BETTER

1 Comparing countries   comparative adjectives

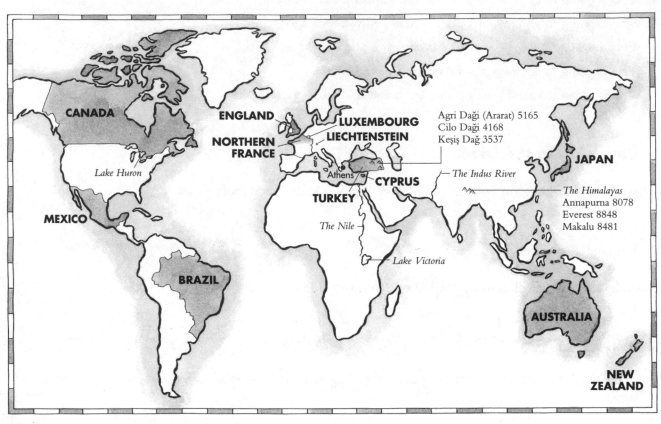

Choose comparative adjectives from the box to complete the sentences. For some sentences you can choose a country or city.

greener	wetter	colder	bigger	longer	more polluted	larger
smaller	more crowded	drier	higher	hotter		

Example: *Brazil is big but Canada is bigger.*

1. Australia is big but Canada is b.................. .

2. Luxembourg is small but Liechtenstein ....

3. The mountains in Turkey are high but the Himalayas ....

4. The Indus river is long but the Nile ....

5. Lake Huron in Canada is large but Lake Victoria in Africa ....

6. England is cold in winter but .... is ....

7. Cyprus is hot in summer but ....

8. Mexico is dry in summer but ....

9. Northern France is wet in winter but .... is ....

10. New Zealand is green but ....

11. Japan's cities are crowded but ....'s c................ are ....

12. Athens is polluted but .... is ....

2 I'm older than my brother

Write *T* (true) or *F* (false) in the boxes.

1. a bit noisier = a lot noisier ☐   4. a lot livelier = much livelier ☐

2. much slimmer = a lot slimmer ☐   5. a bit more reserved = much more reserved ☐

3. a little shyer = a bit shyer ☐

Choose five of the adjectives in the box. Write sentences comparing yourself to friends or relatives. Show your teacher, if you like.

Example: *I'm a bit slimmer than my brother.*
          I'm much taller than Maria.

old	young	short	tall	thin	slim	intelligent	pretty	shy
outgoing	reserved	quiet	noisy	lively				

3 Best and worst

Complete the sentences about your life. Show them to your teacher, if you like.

1. My worst holiday was when I went to .... (country/place) in 19...... .

2. My best teacher at school was .... (name)

3. My w.......... job was when I was a .... (occupation) in
   .... (year)

4. My b.......... toy was a .... (type of toy)

5. My worst experience in another country was when I ....
   .... in .... (country)

6. My .... friend at school was called ....

7. My best .... was .... (you choose!)

8. My .... (you choose!)

Write about a special person in your life. Choose your own superlatives.

Example: *Anna is the finest, richest, most intelligent, most sensitive, funniest and tidiest person I know.*

.... is the ....
.... person I know.

Write about a different sort of person you know! Choose your own superlatives.

Example: *Peter is the noisiest, dirtiest and most unpleasant person I know.*

.... is the ....
.... person I know.

4 Good or bad?

Here are some of the words from Unit 13 in the Class Book. Put each into an appropriate square. Look at the two examples first.

	Usually good (+)	Usually bad (−)	Good and bad (+ −)
for people	*outgoing*		
for countries or cities			
for countries, cities or people		*noisy*	

crowded	outgoing	noisy	lively	polluted	cheap	exciting
friendship	slim	reserved	optimistic	tidy	atmosphere	

Which are the two nouns in the box of words?

5 Comparing pictures

A
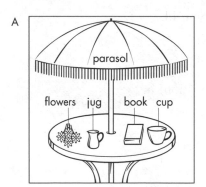

B
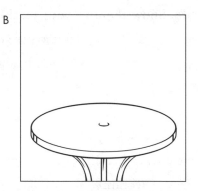

📖 Listen to a learner comparing picture A and picture B. Draw picture B.

6 Shall I compare you to ...

📖 Listen to three people making comparisons. Fill in the blanks:

1. Shall I compare you to a ....? You are .... and more mysterious.

2. Shall I compare you to a mango? You are .... and more ....

3. Shall I compare you to a ....? You are more calculating and more ....

What can you compare your favourite person to? A summer's day? A winter's day? An apple? Use this beginning:

Shall I compare you to a ....? You are more .... and more

....

Complete the sentences.

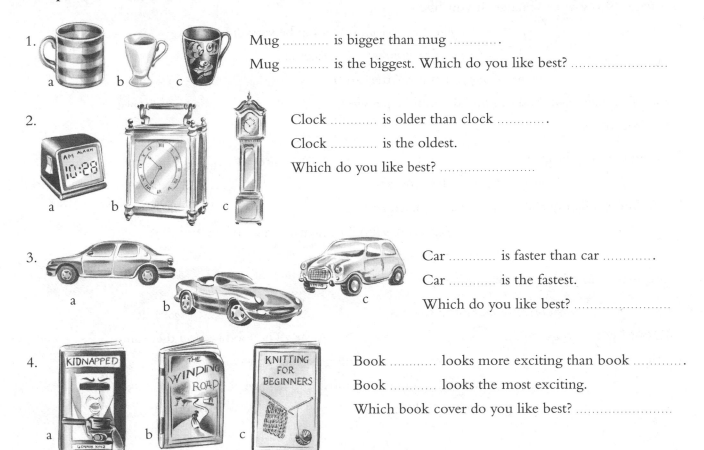

1. Mug .... is bigger than mug ....

   Mug .... is the biggest. Which do you like best? ....

2. Clock .... is older than clock ....

   Clock .... is the oldest.

   Which do you like best? ....

3. Car .... is faster than car ....

   Car .... is the fastest.

   Which do you like best? ....

4. Book .... looks more exciting than book ....

   Book .... looks the most exciting.

   Which book cover do you like best? ....

8 English sayings　　　　　　　　　　　　　　　reading

Here are some English sayings, but they are mixed up.
Match the beginnings with the right endings.

1. A chain is only as strong as	the hardest.
2. The best things in life are	never happen.
3. Least said	no advice at all.
4. The sooner	its weakest link.
5. The best kind of advice is	the better.
6. The first step is always	free.
7. The worst may	makes the biggest sound.
8. An empty vessel	soonest mended.

Now match each saying with one of these interpretations:

a. Be optimistic; expect good things to happen, not bad things.
b. It's best not to talk too much about a problem. Don't say anything and you can solve a problem more quickly.
c. It's often hard to start doing something, then it gets easier as you do it.
d. Because someone talks a lot, it doesn't mean they are very intelligent. Stupid people often talk a lot of rubbish!
e. Don't give advice to other people. They may not like it.
f. When you are working with other people, everyone has to help each other. When one person doesn't do the work well, the whole thing is not so good.
g. Things like love and friendship are the best things in life, because you can't buy them with money.
h. Don't wait. Do things quickly.

Compare prices at different shops and restaurants in your city or town by completing the gaps. Show your teacher, if you like.

In .... (*your city or town*), prices can be very different.

.... (*name of an item*) is/are cheaper at ....

.... (*name of shop*) than it is / they are at ....

(*name of different shop*). You can find the most expensive .... (*same*

item) probably at ....

You can buy the cheapest .... (*another item*) at ....

.... (*shop*). It costs/They cost about .... (*price*),

but to buy the best quality you can pay as much as .... (*price*).

The .... (*superlative adjective*) cinema tickets cost about

.... , but at some cinemas, such as ....

(*name of cinema*), you pay more.

The .... expensive restaurant in town is .... (*name*). It's

OK, but I prefer to go to .... (*name*). The food is good there and

much .... (*comparative adjective*). I never go to ....

.... (*another restaurant*). It's quite expensive and has the ....

.... food (*superlative adjective*).

10 Visual dictionary

Complete the visual dictionary for Unit 13 on page 136.

A Answer the questions and think of reasons.

Which did you find the easiest exercise to do in this unit?

Which did you find the most difficult?

Which did you find the most interesting exercise in this unit?

Which exercise helped your learning the most?

....

B Is there a difference between comparatives and superlatives in your language?

C Write *Y* (yes) or *N* (no) in the boxes next to these statements:

1. Comparison in my language is more complex than in English. ☐
2. I think it is easier for a learner to learn all the different forms of the comparative adjective in my language than it is to learn them in English. ☐
3. My language also has unusual comparative and superlative forms for *good* and *bad*. ☐

14

A SPIRIT OF ADVENTURE

1 I've started

Complete these tables by putting in the correct letters.

Positive statements	Negative statements	Questions
I'_ _ started.	I haven'_ started.	Have you finished?
You've start_ _ .	You haven't start_ _ .	H_ _ she/he/it finished?
He/she/it'_ started.	She/he/it _ _ _ n't started.	Ha_ _ they/we finish_ _?
We'_ _ started.	We _ _ _ _ _' started.	
_ _ _ _'ve started.	They _ _ _ _ _'t started.	

2 The taxi's arrived

What is the person saying in each picture? Choose some suitable words to complete the sentences.

1. It's stopped raining.
2. The taxi's a................
3. I've .... my car keys.
4. They' .... my ....

⊡ Listen. Compare your answers with the ones on the recording.

Choose a or b:

It's stopped raining in picture 1 is the short form of:
a. It is stopped raining.   b. It has stopped raining.

3 Have you ever slept all night on a beach?

short answers; present perfect

Listen to these questions and write in the answers you hear.

Questions   *Answers*

1. Have you ever slept all night on a beach?   ....
2. Have you ever visited a camel farm?   ....
3. Have you ever played basketball?   ....
4. Have you ever spent some time in hospital?   ....
5. Have you ever stayed in an expensive hotel? ....
6. Have you ever been to Nepal?   ....
7. Have you ever lost all your money?   ....

Listen again and say the answers for you.

4 Has she? No, she hasn't

present perfect

1	2
3	4

Write the names of different relatives or good friends in the four boxes.
Now write answers to these questions.

Examples: *Has (John) started a new job recently? No, he hasn't / Yes, he has.*
Have (John and Maria) ever been overseas? No, they haven't / Yes, they have.

Has 1 started a new job recently? ....

Have 2 and 4 ever met? ....

Has 3 bought a new car recently? ....

Has 2 changed a lot in the last few years? ....

Have 1 and 3 ever been overseas? ....

Imagine one of your friends is with you now. Ask your friend three *have you* questions.

1. Have you ....?
2. Have you ....?
3. Have you ....?

5 Sports

vocabulary

Put these sports into the appropriate box. Add one or two others.

scuba diving   golf
soccer   karate
horse riding   tennis
cricket   motor racing
basketball   ballooning
ice hockey   skydiving
sailing

Sports with a ball	Water sports	Sports in the air	Other sports

6 I haven't had time

Listen to the example. Mark the words in the answer that have the strongest sound.

Example: *Have you done your homework?*
I'm sorry but I haven't had time.

Listen and say the same answer to the other questions. Remember to change your answer when you hear *she* or *they*.

Listen again to the questions and answers.

7 She's suffering from stress

Look at the example, then write the other health problems next to a suitable arrow.

cold   broken leg
headache
pain in the stomach
sore throat
cough

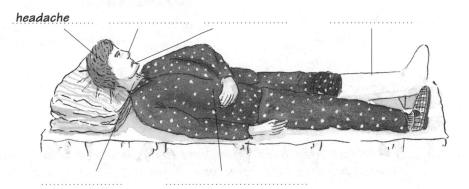

Listen to three short conversations in the doctor's office. Fill in the missing information.

Patient 1 is a man. He's got a ....

Patient 2 is a woman. She's got a ....

Patient 3 is a woman. She feels ....

What about you? How are you today? Which of the two answers is right for you?

a. I'm very well, thank you.
or
b. I'm not very well. I've got ....

8 Have you ever seen sumo wrestling?

Listen to two people talking about the sports events that they have seen or been to. Complete the tables.

	Man		Woman	
	Has he been to / seen it? Yes/No	Did he enjoy it? Yes/No / Yes and no	Has she been to / seen it? Yes/No	Did she enjoy it? Yes/No / Yes and no
soccer	....	....	....	....
cricket	....	....	....	....
horse racing	....	....	....	....
skiing	....	....	....	....
sumo wrestling	....	....	....	....

Which of the sports in the visual dictionary on page 137 have you been to or seen on TV? Write sentences like this:

I've been to a .... match/meeting. It was ....

....

I've seen .... on TV. It was ....

9 Progress reports

Read this report on the progress of Pehr. He is learning English.

PROGRESS REPORT

Name: *Pehr Andresen*   Level: *1*   Term: *1*

Nationality: *Swedish*   Teachers: *Jean Ure / Colin Forbes*

General Progress: *Pehr has made good progress. He has worked hard in class and has made lots of friends. He is popular with other students and uses his English all the time.*

Grammar: *He has tried hard to improve his accuracy and has spent some of his spare time on grammar practice. He sometimes finds it difficult to use the verb tenses accurately.*

Listening: *Pehr finds listening easy and this has made it easier for him to improve his basic conversation skills. He likes listening to the radio and this has also helped him.*

Speaking: *His spoken English has improved a lot because he enjoys speaking to his teachers and his friends. His pronunciation is good but he has had a bit of trouble with intonation.*

Reading: *Pehr doesn't enjoy reading and has not tried very hard in reading classes. He has not realised that reading is an important skill and that a good reader can often write better formal English. As he wants to go to an English-speaking university one day, academic writing is going to be very important*

Writing: *Pehr has worked hard to improve his writing and has enjoyed writing simple letters to his pen friend in New Zealand. He has also increased his vocabulary by keeping a diary in English. He has had difficulty in using expressions like 'in the end' and 'eventually'.*

Homework: *He has completed homework regularly but sometimes he has presented work in an incomplete state.*

Signed: *Jean Ure   Colin Forbes*   Date: *14/6/95*

Now complete these sentences:

1. Pehr has made good progress in ....

2. He has had a few problems with ....

3. He has tried to improve ....

4. He hasn't worked very hard on his ....

10 My progress report

Write your own progress report. Use some of the language in the report you read or some from the box if you like.

> I have made excellent/good/quite good/fairly good/satisfactory/disappointing progress.
> I still have difficulty with …
> I still don't understand …
> I haven't spent enough time on …
> I'm really pleased with my progress in …

11 Visual dictionary

Complete the visual dictionary for Unit 14 on page 137.

12 Reflections

Complete this postcard to an old English teacher or English-speaking friend. Choose words for *a*, *b*, *c* and *d* from the box. Show the postcard to your teacher if you like.

Dear ....,
I hope this card is a nice surprise. You wanted to
know about my English lessons.
Well I have now completed .... units/weeks of
(a)................................. I've found it easy to
(b)......................... English because
....
On the other hand, I've found it difficult to
(c)........................... English because
....
The books I am using are (d)........................... .
My teacher's name is ....
She's/He's ....
I hope you are well. Write when you have
some time and tell me about ....
....
All the best,

> a. my English book/course
> b. speak/write/understand/read
> c. speak/read/write/listen to
> d. great/OK/a bit boring

15

DOES BEING TIDY SAVE TIME?

1 Questions and answers

Here are some questions and answers. Complete the questions.

Example: *Do you dislike* working in an untidy place?
Oh, yes. I hate working in an untidy place. I always tidy my desk before starting work.

1. Q: Do you keep ....?
   A: Yes, I do. I'm always making lists for everything – shopping, things to do at work. It stops me from forgetting things.

2. Q: Do you enjoy ....?
   A: Oh, absolutely. I not only enjoy having a deadline, I can't seem to start anything without one.

3. Q: Do you like ....?
   A: Yes, I do. Writing things down in a diary is important in my job, but I also have a diary to plan my life at home. I write everything down, absolutely everything.

4. Q: Do you keep ....?
   A: No. I never forget appointments. Never.

5. Q: Do you prefer .... immediately?
   A: Of course. As soon as I receive the bill, I open it, get out my cheque book and pay. Leaving bills is a dangerous thing, I think.

6. Q: Do you like ....?
   A: I do, yes. Knowing exactly how much money I've got is important to me, so I look at all my bank statements very carefully.

▭▭ Listen to the questions and answers, and see if your questions were like those on the recording.

Answer the questions yourself. How many *yes* answers have you got?

▭▭ Listen to the recording for your profile.

2 I keep forgetting things

Complete this short letter to a magazine about the things you keep forgetting or losing. Use the box for ideas if you like.

birthdays	keys
(to) lock the car door	
(to) feed the cat	
(to) get petrol	
bag	umbrella

Dear John,

I'm hoping you can help me. I'm a very busy person. I never seem to have much time and so I keep forgetting things. I keep forgetting ....
I also keep forgetting to ....
Another problem I have is losing things. For example, I keep losing my .... , and I keep losing .... as well.
Can you please help me?

Yours,

3 Before going to sleep

What's the first or last thing you do? Think of answers to these questions.

1. What's the first thing you do before starting work in the morning?
2. What's the last thing you do before going to sleep?
3. What's the first thing you do after eating your breakfast?
4. What's the last thing you do before leaving work?
5. What's the first thing you do after getting home from a long holiday?
6. What's the last thing you do in the house before going away for a holiday?
7. What's the first thing you say after picking up the phone?

▭ Listen to people giving answers. Which questions are they answering?

Speaker 1: Question ......

Speaker 2: Question ......

Speaker 3: Question ......

Speaker 4: Question ......

▭ Listen and check your answers.

4 Companies always want people with experience

Put the appropriate *-ing* word from the box into each space in the article.

| putting   finding   writing   going to   buying   making |

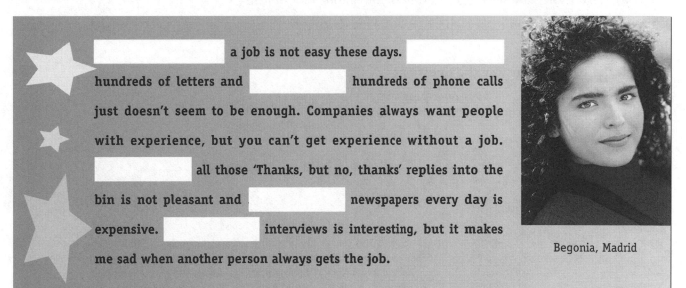

_____ a job is not easy these days. _____ hundreds of letters and _____ hundreds of phone calls just doesn't seem to be enough. Companies always want people with experience, but you can't get experience without a job. _____ all those 'Thanks, but no, thanks' replies into the bin is not pleasant and _____ newspapers every day is expensive. _____ interviews is interesting, but it makes me sad when another person always gets the job.

Begonia, Madrid

5 You put waste paper in the bin

Match each word or expression in the box on the left with one from the box on the right.

Example: *envelope – letter*

| computer   diary   desk
bin   envelope
photocopier   mug | waste paper   letter   disk
appointment   coffee
office chair   sheets of paper |

 Listen to people talking about less usual ways of using the things in the pictures. What do they say each thing is useful for or handy for?

Old business cards are handy for:	An old mug is handy for:	Old telephone books are useful for:
1.	1.	1. ....
2.	2.	2. ....
3.		3. ....

A Tick the appropriate boxes. Use a dictionary to help you.

1. Which forms of information do you regularly read or listen to?
   newspapers ☐   journals ☐   books ☐   magazines ☐   computer data ☐
   TV ☐   radio ☐   surveys ☐   reports ☐   memos ☐

2. How do you cope with the increasing amounts of information?
   Do you read more and more? ☐   Or do you ignore a lot of it? ☐

3. Does more information make you better at taking decisions?
   Yes. ☐   No. ☐

B Read the text and answer the questions.

1. In the text find two other ways of coping with information.
2. Is the writer's answer to Question 3 above *yes* or *no*?

INFOMANIA

There is a saying 'knowledge is power'. Well, in the 1990s that is not true. The problem is there is just so much information these days that it's impossible really to know very much at all. Take these facts, for example. In the 14th century the Sorbonne in Paris had 1338 books and was the largest library in the world. In 1993 there were about 1000 new books printed in English every week.

On Sunday, November 13, 1987, *The New York Times* had 1612 pages!

And it's not only books and newspapers – there are reports, computer data bases, journals, magazines, TV and radio. Computers seem to make the problem worse. They give us plenty of organised information but they don't help us with understanding. Many people seem to believe in choice. They say, the more information or knowledge we have, the more choices we have. Wrong. The more choice we have, the more anxious we seem to be about making bad decisions.

What can we do with these mountains of information? One choice is to read everything about everything. Another choice is to ignore everything.

One of my friends puts everything unimportant on his desk and puts everything important on the floor. Another puts all his office papers into bags and then writes the date on each bag. The bags go to the garden shed or the garage. If he doesn't open a bag by the end of six months, he throws the bag out.

Come to think of it, reading this text is probably not a good way of spending your time, so why don't you go and read a poem – that's a much better form of communication!

C Which words in the text are opposites of these?

1. important – ....

2. better – ....

3. to take notice of – ....

D Which sentences in the text mean the same as these?

1. The great amount of information actually makes it difficult for people to build real knowledge about things.

....

2. Having more information and more choices makes us worried in case we make wrong decisions.

....

8 I hate working late

Complete these two paragraphs for a newspaper article about work. You can use the ideas in the box to help you. Show your teacher, if you like.

> *in*: the evening   unfriendly offices   cities   big offices   friendly places
> *with*: unfriendly people   friendly people   efficient people   quiet people
>   men and women   young people
> *for*: lazy managers   kind managers   a good company   a small salary

I don't like working in .... and I
hate working with .... Most of
all, I dislike working for ....

I love working in .... and I like
working with .... I especially
like working for ....

Now write two more paragraphs. Choose your own words after *in/at* and *with*. Give a reason after *because*.

I like/dislike spending time in/at .... and I love/hate spending

time with .... because ....

9 Visual dictionary

Complete the visual dictionary for Unit 15 on page 137.

10 Reflections

English uses verbs ending in *-ing* in many different ways. Here are some of the ways:

I like **working** with my friends.
I keep **forgetting** to pay my bills on time!
Storing things is a problem in my small office.
I tidy my desk before **starting** work.

Think about your own language. How do you say these things in your language? Does your language use an *-ing* form in a way that is similar to English?

16

OUR NEIGHBOURHOOD

1 I saw, I've seen   revision of verb forms

Fill in the missing verb forms in this table of common irregular verbs.

Infinitive	*Past simple*	*Present perfect*
to go	I went	....
....	I saw	I've seen
to eat	I ate	....
to take	....	I've taken
to make	....	I've made
....	I did	I've done
to find	....	I've found
to have	I had	....
to buy	....	....

Now write down one thing you did yesterday and two things you've bought so far this week.

I .... yesterday.

I've .... and .... this week.

2 I've just packed my suitcase   present perfect with *just*

Look at the line. The person on the phone is talking to a friend. What's she saying?
Write sentences like the example.

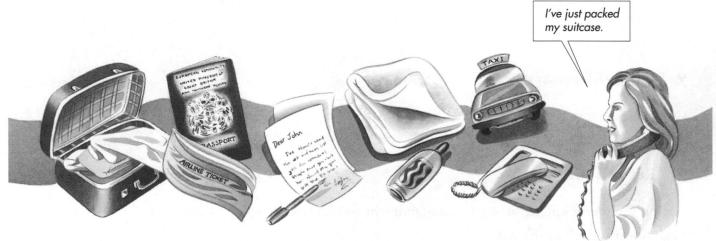

I've just packed
my suitcase.

1. I've just checked my ....
2. I've just .... a letter to ....
3. I've just ....
4. I've just .... for a taxi.

3 No, not yet

Write four questions with *yet* using the words in a to d.

Example: You / to pay / the .... bill (type of bill)?
Have you paid the gas bill yet?

a. Elena / to see / .... (name of film)?

b. Your brother / to phone / .... (name of person or company)?

c. Carlos and Miguel / to buy / .... (something from the shops)?

d. You / to read / .... (name of a daily newspaper)?

4 A watch is a thing

A Match the first part of each sentence with the rest of its unusual definition.

1. A dentist is a person   a. where you leave your money and your money leaves you.
2. A restaurant is a place   b. that drives you to the bank.
3. A doctor is a person   c. who knows every part of you.
4. A car is a thing   d. that always has time for you.
5. A bank is a place   e. where most people finish their courses.
6. A watch is a thing   f. who gets richer every time you open your mouth.

B Write in the missing part of these definitions:

1. .... who is your aunt's child.

2. .... where you can buy almost anything.

3. .... that people read in the morning and throw away at night.

Now write your own definitions for these:

a teacher   a politician   a television   a kitchen

5 Your neighbourhood

Which of these buildings and places are less than two kilometres from where you live? Write the word for each item inside or outside the circle to show where it is.

swimming pool   farm supermarket   bank factory   park petrol station   small shop church or mosque   hospital restaurant   cinema market   post office

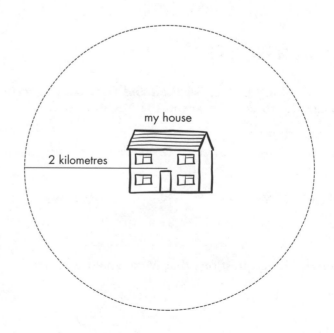

6 It's the petrol station

A 🔲 Listen and repeat. Mark a circle (o) above the part of the expression with the strong sound. Listen to the examples first.

Examples: *The univ*°*ersity*
 The dep°*artment store*

1. the library
2. the petrol station
3. the tourist office
4. the railway station
5. the shopping centre

B 🔲 Look at the street map.
Say answers to the questions on the recording.
Now listen again and check your answers.

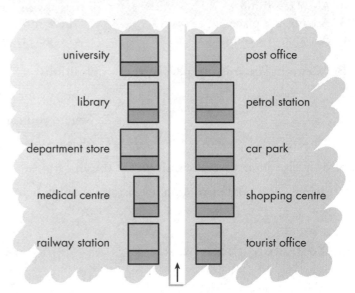

university		post office
library		petrol station
department store		car park
medical centre		shopping centre
railway station		tourist office

7 Just the headlines

🔲 Mike is asking Jackie, Stephen and Dave some questions about this week. Listen and correct the three mistakes in the Yes/No notes.

Have you ...	read the paper?	been to the bank?	been shopping?	had a holiday?	paid the electricity bill?
Jackie:	No	Yes	No	No	No
Stephen:	Yes	No	Yes	Yes	Yes
Dave:	Yes	No	No	No	No

Write down three questions that Mike asked with *yet*.

1. ....?
2. ....?
3. ....?

A What is a garage sale? Look through the newspaper article quickly and find the answer.

The text mentions some advantages and disadvantages of garage sales. Read these two lists, then read the article. Tick the ones that are mentioned in the article.

Advantages
They're fun. ☐
You make money. ☐
You have less junk. ☐
They're helpful in hard times. ☐
You learn about selling. ☐
You meet new people. ☐
You can find bargains. ☐

Disadvantages
You can end up buying stolen goods. ☐
People are giving less to charities. ☐
There are legal problems. ☐
People are becoming too selfish. ☐
You can't get your money back easily. ☐
People take things without paying. ☐

GARAGE SALES — A GOOD IDEA?

Garage sales have arrived from the United States and have become popular in Australia and England in the past few years. But there are some problems. Reporter Philip Macdonald looks at both sides.

Every weekend thousands of people go to garage sales in towns and cities in Australia and England. People bring all the things they want to sell from their house and garden. They put them in their garage with a price label and then advertise the sale in the newspaper. Other people in the city then come and buy.

Charity organisations are not happy about garage sales. They are losing many second-hand things that they could sell and they have less money for their charity work. They say that there are garage sales even in wealthy suburbs. People are becoming more selfish and giving less to charity organisations.

There are a number of legal problems with garage sales. When you sell something that is in bad condition, like an old chair, there could be legal problems in the case of an accident. Also, it isn't easy for buyers to get their money back when they buy something that doesn't work very well.

On the positive side, garage sales can be fun and they help people to learn about selling things. In difficult economic times it is easy to see why garage sales are popular, because you can earn $500 from the sale of the junk you no longer want in your house.

So, here are a few ideas for you:

What to sell –
things you haven't used for two years or more.

Where to sell –
a clean garage close to the road, or in a big tent or on a lawn.

Selling price –
20–30% of the price of a new one.

Best time to sell –
Saturday in spring or autumn.

Advertising –
local newspaper; also make sure there are nice, clear signs in the road on the day of your sale.

B Match the expressions with appropriate meanings or pictures.

Example: *3 – e (Charities are organisations which give money to poor or sick people.)*

Expressions
1. junk
2. second-hand
3. charities
4. legal
5. tent
6. sign

Meanings

a.

b.

c. not new
d. about the law
e. organisations which give money to poor or sick people
f. things you want to throw away or sell

Write examples under these headings of items for sale in these advertisements.

Vehicles	*Clothes*	*Musical instruments*	*Electronic equipment*	*Animals*
....	....	....	....	....
....	....	....	....	....
....	....	....	....	....

GUITARS (2)
good condition $75 the lot
Alberton 603 7120

IBM compatible
with VGA monitor,
30 mb hard disk. $300.
Unley 339 2011

Men's leather jacket,
medium size, grey, never
worn $180.
FORRESTON 772 3541

BABY DWARF RABBITS,
white, 7 weeks old.
Coromandel Valley
407 2996

**JVC 3 in 1
stereo system,**
excellent condition with
table. $300 negotiable.
Glenelg 405 5528

ANGLO ARAB CHESTNUT MARE,
15.1 hh, 11 years old, with papers, good to
show, shoe and good in traffic, regrettable
sale – to good home only. $550.
Bakalava 458 6670

Wedding dress
*Size 8, white lace and satin, off
shoulder style, too beautiful to
describe, worth $1400, sell $600 or
near offer.*
Smithfield 605 9547

Toyota Corolla hatchback
November 1989, 5 speed, air, excellent
condition $11999 or near offer.
Largs Bay 663 3071

Think of two things you want to sell. Write advertisements for them.

boxed as new, cost £180, will
281   accept £140 ono. — 02379
506543.

Oft x
roxi-
. —

£40.   **SHEDS (TOPWOOD),** Wendy-

7ft
do
sid
thr
exce
cer
dra
02

Push-
new,
ncing

TELEVISION/VIDEO CABINET
teak effect, swivel top, £20. —
02379 758950.

GREEN DRALON large three
piece Suite, £450. — 02379

ME
tools
appr
Stora
garag

ALL
items
shee
Foot
£1

10 Visual dictionary

Complete the visual dictionary for Unit 16 on page 138.

11 Reflections

Which of these are true for you and which are false? Put *T* or *F* in the boxes.

1. I haven't listened to English on my radio yet. ☐
2. I haven't spoken to English people in my city yet. ☐
3. I haven't written a letter in English to a friend yet. ☐

Write about two ways you are going to use your English in the future.

1. I'm going to ....
2. I'm going to ....

17

IT'S WORTH DOING WELL

1 Thinking about adverbs and adjectives

A Complete the sentences and add examples to help you remember.

1. Adjectives are used with nouns. Examples: a good book, a ....

....

2. Adverbs are used with .... Examples: She eats quickly, He drinks

....

3. To form many adverbs, add .... to the adjective. Examples: complete –

completely, ... – ....

4. Some adverbs are different. Example: good – ....

B Are adjectives and adverbs used in the same way in your language?
Translate into your first language:

1. She's a good pianist.

....

2. She plays the piano very well.

....

3. He's a careful driver.

....

4. He drives carefully.

....

2 I sing badly

Answer the questionnaire. Choose *a*, *b* or *c*.

I eat	For work I usually dress	I sing
❏ a. cheaply.	❏ a. formally.	❏ a. beautifully.
❏ b. expensively.	❏ b. informally.	❏ b. badly.
❏ c. healthily.	❏ c. badly.	❏ c. occasionally.
I usually drive	**I speak English**	**I cook**
❏ a. carefully.	❏ a. well.	❏ a. quickly.
❏ b. quickly.	❏ b. slowly.	❏ b. efficiently.
❏ c. well.	❏ c. badly.	❏ c. badly.

Now write sentences about three friends, like this example.

Example: *Helga sings beautifully. She also drives carefully and speaks English slowly.*

3 I'm generally an untidy person

Write sentences about yourself. Use the adjectives in the box.

neat	tidy	polite	untidy	intelligent	clever	careful	patient
efficient	slow	noisy	quick	confident	quiet	easy	

Write your sentences like this:

I'm generally/usually/often a .... (adjective) person.

I .... (verb) .... (adverb), and I .... (verb)

.... (adverb). .... (adjective).

Example: *I'm generally a <u>neat</u> person. I eat <u>neatly</u>, and I work <u>neatly</u>. My flat is very <u>neat</u>.*

4 Opposites

Fill in the missing words.

Adjective	Opposite	Adverb	Opposite
tidy	untidy	tidily	....
good	bad	....	....
....	slow	quickly	....
skilful	clumsy	....	....
patient	....	....	impatiently
....	careless	carefully	....
noisy	....	....	quietly
....	unnatural	....	....

5 Describe a good language learner

Which of these things do you think describe good language learners? Put *Y* (*yes*) or
N (*no*) in the boxes.

Good language learners:

1. use the new language confidently. ☐

2. explore and try to understand more about the language. ☐

3. aren't interested in people. ☐

4. like to understand why people say things in certain ways. ☐

5. take their learning seriously. ☐

6. learn patiently. ☐

7. know that learning a language means having a good time. ☐

⬚⬚ Listen to two teachers talking about good language learners. Tick the things above
(1–7) that they mention.

A Before reading the text, think about using a video camera.
Imagine you buy a new video camera. Tick the topics that you think the instruction
book probably discusses.

1. how to hold the camera
2. how to take interesting shots
3. how to take care of the camera
4. how to check all the equipment
5. how to make a good quality
   television programme
6. how to understand all the buttons
   on the camera

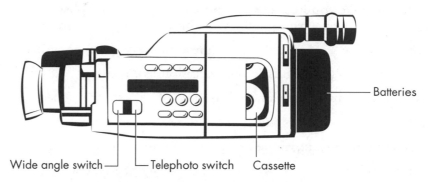

Wide angle switch ——— └— Telephoto switch   Cassette

Read part of an instruction book. Which of the topics are mentioned?

Instruction
manual

SUGGESTIONS FOR GOOD RECORDING

Making films with a video camera is becoming more and more popular as a hobby these days. Here is some help for you to make sure that you use your camera confidently and efficiently.

PREPARATION

It's a good idea to watch television programmes to get an idea of how they begin and how they end. Check all the camera equipment and make sure it all works properly. Make sure you have several cassettes and batteries because recording often takes more time than you expect.

RECORDING

Before you start recording, plan each shot. Think carefully about the most important subject in the picture. Is it a person, a building, some scenery? It is very tiring to watch images that shake, so when you hold the camera in your hand and move about, keep your body in a stable position and hold the camera securely.

When moving the camera up and down (tilting) or across (panning), do so slowly. Don't pan or tilt too frequently. Except for special shots of great interest, the usual length of one shot is from five to ten seconds. Shots that are too long become boring, and when they are too short the viewer gets dizzy.

Make sure the subject is in the centre of the picture. Be careful not to put your hand or fingers in front of the camera when recording.

Try not to take the same kind of shots again and again. Change from wide angle to telephoto from time to time. Be careful not to take shots while moving or while in dangerous places. Safety is the most important thing.

PRECAUTIONS

Do not use the camera in the rain. Handle the camera gently at all times. Don't point the camera directly into the sunlight. Don't leave the camera in a hot car. Store the camera in a dry place.

B Which of these statements mean the same as statements in the text? Put *S* (same) or
D (different) in the boxes.

1. Make sure all the equipment works well. ☐
2. People get tired of watching pictures that move too much. ☐
3. Very interesting shots are often of 5 to 10 seconds. ☐
4. Don't repeat the same shots time after time. ☐
5. Always handle the camera carefully. ☐
6. Don't point at the camera on sunny days. ☐

C Which of these expressions is not used in the text to describe filming with a video camera?

1. tilt   2. recording   3. pan   4. photograph   5. shot   6. telephoto   7. wide angle

7 I'm a great photographer

writing

Everyone takes photos. How good are your photographs?
Write one or two paragraphs. Use these outlines or write your own.

My photos are .... (great, not very good) because I use my camera
.... (regularly, only occasionally). I .... (plan, don't plan) my
shots very carefully. My camera is a/an .... (cheap, expensive, complex) one
and is .... (easy, hard) to use.

I can remember some of the best photos I have taken. One is of .... (a friend,
a place) called .... I like the shot because it ....
....

Another of my favourite photos is of .... I think it is
....

Photography is not my favourite hobby but I enjoy taking photos when I ....
.... (travel, stay with friends, go to weddings or parties).

8 Visual dictionary

Complete the visual dictionary for Unit 17 on page 139.

9 Reflections

Think about how you learn languages.

What things do you learn quickly and easily?

....

What things do you learn slowly?

....

Why?

....

What can you do to improve?

....

Think of the ways you are studying. What things are making it difficult for you to learn
confidently and efficiently?

....

What can you do to change those things?

....

....

18

ON YOUR TRAVELS

Write sentences to show what each sign says you should or shouldn't do. The first one has been done for you.

1. *This sign means you shouldn't drive faster than 60 km per hour.*

6.    ....
....

2.   *You shouldn't* ....
....

7.    ....
....

3.   *You should* ....
....

8.   ....
....

4.   ....
....
....

9.   ....
....

5. Mon–Sat
    8am–6pm
    Waiting limited
    to 30 minutes
....
....

Complete the sentence beginnings in column 1 by choosing an expression from column 2. Then mark each sentence O, G or NO.

Example: *O* .... *I have to get a new passport.* (Obligation: necessary)
          G .... *You should take a good book.* (Good idea)
          NO .... *You don't have to go by car.* (No obligation: not necessary)

Column 1

1. .... I have to get ....
2. .... You should go ....
3. .... He doesn't have to drink ....
4. .... She has to catch ....
5. .... We don't have to show ....
6. .... They shouldn't forget ....

Column 2

bottled water.
to gate 3.
the train.
our passports.
their tickets.
a visa.

---

3 Should I carry cash?

Read the answers, then complete the questions appropriately.

Example: *Should I* <u>carry cash or should I take travellers' cheques</u> ?
You should definitely take travellers' cheques, they're safer.

1. Q: Which gate should ....?
   A: Passengers should go to gate number 11.

2. Q: Where ....?
   A: Travellers should apply for visas at the embassy.

3. Q: When ....?
   A: She should get a visa two weeks before travelling.

4. Q: What kind of water ....?
   A: To be safe, you should only drink bottled water.

5. Q: Do we ....?
   A: Yes, all travellers from your country have to have a visa.

6. Q: Does he ....?
   A: He doesn't have to have a return ticket, but it can be useful.

7. Q: Do we ....?
   A: Yes, you all have to go through Customs.

8. Q: What ....?
   A: She has to fill in her name, her address and her passport number.

9. Q: Where ....?
   A: Sign at the bottom of the form.

10. Q: Can I ....?
    A: I'm sorry, but the plane is full. You'll have to stay where you are, I'm afraid.

4 The travel agent's special offer

⬚ Read the dialogue. Some of it is missing. Then listen and write in the missing parts.

CUSTOMER: Do you have a half price ticket to Africa?

TRAVEL AGENT: ....?

CUSTOMER: Yes, on TV you advertised half price travel to Africa.

TRAVEL AGENT: ....?

CUSTOMER: Yes, it was an offer for everyone over 45.

TRAVEL AGENT: ....?

CUSTOMER: Yes, I'm 55 and so are my five friends.

TRAVEL AGENT: ....?

CUSTOMER: Yes, so can we have five half price special travel offer tickets for Africa, please?

TRAVEL AGENT: Sorry, the offer finished five days ago.

CUSTOMER: That's not very fair, we'll have to travel full fare now.

TRAVEL AGENT: That's life, I'm afraid!

⬚ Now listen again. This time, you say the customer's lines.

Put the expressions in the box into the right column.

Go to	*Go to the*
....	....
....	....
....	....
....	....
....	....
....	....
....	....
....	....

embassy	Egypt	station
South America	São Paulo	
United States	gate 7	
travel agency	check-in counter	
work	Middle East	exit
school	Tokyo	bed
platform 8	hotel	
duty-free shop		

Listen to the sentences on the recording and check your answers. The sentences use different forms of the verb *to go*.

6 Fill in the form

PLEASE PRINT

1. FAMILY NAME	
2. CHRISTIAN OR GIVEN NAMES	

3. COUNTRY OF CITIZENSHIP		4. PASSPORT NUMBER	

5. COUNTRY OF BIRTH		6. DATE OF BIRTH	Day Month Year / /

7. SEX Male ❑ Female ❑	8. MARITAL STATUS	❑ Never Married ❑ Now Married	❑ Widowed ❑ Divorced

9. Please answer ONE of **D** or **E** or **F**

D **Visitor or temporary entrant departing**

1. I have been in Australia this visit for a period of

Years [ ]
Months [ ]
OR
Days [ ]

2. In Australia I spent most time in

(State or City)

3. Country of residence

E **Resident departing temporarily**

INCLUDES persons who came to settle in Australia

1. I intend to stay abroad for a period of

Years [ ]   Months [ ]   OR   Days [ ]

2. Main reason for going abroad *(Please mark ONLY ONE box)*

Student vacation ❑ 1   Visiting relatives ❑ 5
Convention ❑ 2   Holiday ❑ 6
Business ❑ 3   Employment ❑ 7
Accompanying business traveller ❑ 4   Education ❑ 8
                          Other ❑ 9

3. Country in which I shall spend most time

4. In Australia I live in

(State or Territory)

F **Resident departing permanently**

1. Country of future residence

2. In Australia I lived in

(State or Territory)

3. If not born in Australia how long ago did you come to live in Australia?

Years [ ]   Months [ ]

4. Did you intend to SETTLE permanently?

Yes [ ]   No [ ]

10. USUAL OCCUPATION	

11. DEPARTURE DETAILS Date / / day month year	Flight No./ Name of Ship	Airport/ Port

12. COUNTRY IN WHICH I SHALL GET OFF THIS FLIGHT OR SHIP *(ABROAD)*	
	SIGNATURE / / 19

This is an outgoing passenger card for travellers leaving Australia. Listen to the recording and fill in the card for the speaker.

Do you think the following statements are true or false? Put *T* or *F* in the boxes. Use a dictionary to help you.

1. Ways of protecting travellers have not changed much in recent years. ☐
2. Travellers have to have more injections now than in the past. ☐
3. Injections against yellow fever are necessary in some countries. ☐
4. Travellers who have health problems should see their doctor before they travel. ☐
5. There is no help for people who get sick in cars or planes. ☐
6. Travellers should take a bandage with them in case they have accidents. ☐
7. Travellers shouldn't take aspirin with them. ☐
8. Malaria is a danger in some countries and travellers should protect themselves against it. ☐
9. Insect repellent cannot protect travellers against malaria. ☐
10. In some countries, travellers should use tablets to purify the water. ☐

Here are two short texts from a book on how to stay healthy when travelling. Read the texts and check your answers to the true and false statements above.

Healthy travelling

Ways of protecting travellers against disease have changed in recent years. Nowadays, there are not many injections that are absolutely necessary for travel to certain countries – injections against yellow fever are about the only example. However, there are some injections which are still strongly advised for travel to many countries. It is important for anyone travelling to a warm country to get advice from a health centre and to remember not to stay out in the sun.

Some people feel sick in planes or cars. They should ask their doctor about it before they go on their trip. They can now get tablets to make travelling safer and more enjoyable.

If travellers have any health problems, they should discuss them with their doctor before they leave. It is the only way they can be sure of travelling safely.

It is a good idea for travellers to take mild aspirin with them for headache, toothache or in case of small accidents. It is also useful to take a mild cream for insect bites. Travellers going to a country with mosquitoes should put insect repellent on their skin at least twice a day. Tablets against malaria are strongly recommended for some countries, and the traveller has to take the tablets regularly.

Other items which make travelling safer are: an antiseptic cream and a bandage in case of accidents, tablets to purify water, and – something that is not absolutely necessary but often useful – a roll of toilet paper!

It is not an obligation, but health insurance is an important part of health care for travellers.

Using the information in the texts you have read, make lists under these headings:

Travellers have to … *(It's absolutely necessary.)*	*Travellers don't have to …* *(There's no obligation.)*
....	....
....	....
....	....
....	....

Travellers should … *(It's a good idea.)*	Travellers shouldn't … *(It's not a good idea.)*
....	....
....	....
....	....
....	....

9 She should definitely see the Opera House
reading; writing a friendly letter

Imagine that a friend living in a different country writes to you to say their daughter is coming on a holiday to your region. Read the letter.

Dear ....,

Our daughter is going to visit your region in May. Can you give her some advice? What should she plan to see? What kind of clothing should she take? She's thinking of touring the countryside on a bicycle. Is that a good idea? Is it safe, or should she go on buses and trains? She's staying with her pen friend's family. What should she take as a gift? Is there anything she should be careful not to do?
Thank you ever so much for your advice.

Write a letter telling the friend what her daughter should take and what she should do in your region. Are there things she shouldn't do?
Begin like this:

Dear ....,
Thanks for your letter. Here are a few thoughts and ideas. Your daughter should …

10 Visual dictionary

Complete the visual dictionary for Unit 18 on page 140.

11 Reflections

1. Which countries would you like to visit?

....

2. Which other languages would you like to learn?

....

3. Which languages (besides English) do you think your children (or people in 20 years from now) should learn?

....

4. Which cultures would you like to understand a little better?

....

5. Which cultures do you think your children (or people in 20 years from now) should understand better?

....

8 Travellers should use insect repellent   95

19

A LOOK AT LIFE!

1 Would you like to be taller?
Short responses with *would*

Give personal answers to these questions using *Yes, I/they/it would* or *No, I/they/it wouldn't.*

Example: Q: *Would you like to be taller?*
A: *Yes, I would / No, I wouldn't.*

1. Q: Would you like to be thinner?
A: ....

2. Q: Would you like to be lighter?
A: ....

3. Q: Would you like to have longer holidays?
A: ....

4. Q: Would you like to retire early?
A: ....

5. Q: Would your parents or friends like to see you more often?
A: ....
(Remember! *Yes, they would / No, they wouldn't.*)

6. Q: Would your friends like to work every weekend?
A: ....

7. Q: Would your government like to increase the number of people with jobs? (Remember: *it*)
A: ....

8. Q: Would the abolition of cars in your town centre be a good thing?
(Use *it* again, because *abolition* is the subject of the sentence.)
A: ....

9. Q: Would cheaper airfares make you travel more often?
A: ....

10. Q: Would a new home be good for you at the moment?
A: ....

2 What would you like for your birthday?
-'d like + noun

What do you think these people would like for their birthday? Complete the sentences. Use the expressions in the box if you like.

a holiday	a new car
tickets for the theatre	
a nice meal	
a camera	flowers
a box of chocolates	

(you)   I'd like ....

(your sister or friend)   She'd like ....

(your neighbours or parents)   They'd like ....

(your father, brother or friend)   He'd like ....

3 To have more sleep

A Match the verbs with the expressions in the box. Write the expressions in the correct columns.

Examples: <u>to have</u> more time
<u>to be</u> a sky diver

to have	to be	to do
....	....	....
....	....	....
....	....	....
....	....	....
....		

more time   the washing up
in Paris   rich   children
more reading   a sky diver
on holiday   the organising
a holiday   the cooking
more sleep   a lot more travelling

B Write four sentences using your own expressions.

Examples: *I'd like to have a good job / I'd like to be happy / I'd like to learn Greek.*

1. ....
2. ....
3. ....
4. ....

4 Language summary

Complete this table.

Long forms	Short forms
Long forms	*Short forms*
I would like to be young again.	I'd like to be young again.
She .... like to be young again.	She'd like to be young again.
He would like to be young again.	............'...... like to be young again.
We would .... to be young again.	............'...... like to be young again.
You would like to be young again.	You'...... like to be young again.
They would like to be young again.	............'d .... to be young again.
I would not like to be old.	I wouldn't like to be old.
He would .... like to be old.	He wouldn't like to be old.
She .... not like to be old.	She ....n't like to be old.
You would .... like to be old.	You ....n't like to be old.
We .... like to be old.	We .... to be old.
.... like to be old.	They wouldn't ....
Questions	*Answers*
Would you like to be very old?	Yes, I would / No, I wouldn't.
Would she like to be very old?	Yes, she .... / No, she ....
.... have they like to be very old?	Yes, ... / No, ...

How about you? Would you like to be very old? ....

5 Would you like to be more intelligent?

We asked a woman and a man these two questions:

Would you like to be more intelligent?
Would you like to be a man/woman?

CD Listen to their answers and complete the table.

	More intelligent? Yes/No	Why?	Man/woman? Yes/No	Why?
Ian	....	I'm .... intelligent. I'd go	....	I'd be .... to my 5 children.
Lyn	....	I was not one of the .... in the college. I .... inadequate.	....	I'm .... to be a woman. I'm happy to stay as ....

6 I wouldn't like to be a man because ...

Choose either 1 *or* 2 and either 3 *or* 4. Complete the paragraphs you choose.

Example: 2. *Would you like to be a man?*
There are two sides to this question. On the one hand, I wouldn't <u>like</u> to be a man because <u>many men are not good at showing their feelings</u>. Also <u>men don't normally live as long as women</u>. On the other hand, I'd <u>like to be</u> a man because <u>men often have the best jobs and the most freedom</u>.

1. *Would you like to be a woman?*

   There are two sides to this question. On the one hand, I wouldn't .... to be a woman

   because .... Also

   .... On the other hand,

   I'd .... a woman because ....

   ....

or

2. *Would you like to be a man?*

   There are two sides to this question. On the one hand, I wouldn't .... to be a man

   because .... Also ....

   .... On the other hand, I'd ....

   a man because ....

3. *Would you like to be more intelligent?*

   There are two sides to this question. On the one hand, I'd .... to be more intelligent

   because ....

   Also, ... On the other hand,

   I wouldn't .... more intelligent because ....

   ....

or

4. *Would you like to be richer?*

There are two sides to this question. On the one hand, I'd .... to be richer because

.... Also ....

.... On the other hand, I wouldn't ....

richer because ....

---

7 Paris, of course

Read the text and answer the question.

GUESS THE QUESTION

We asked these people the same three questions. Here are their answers. What were the questions?

OMAR

❶ I'd go to Paris, of course.

❷ I'd break down the door with my shoulder and just walk out.

❸ I think it would be disastrous, because most people have to use the car to get to and from work, and the alternatives are not realistic. People would soon get tired of walking around cities, or walking to work, and it's too expensive to develop an urban transportation system for everyone.

HELENA

❶ I'd go to a tropical island, like Tahiti, that has always seemed a romantic sort of place, to me, anyway.

❷ I'd shout until somebody came and unlocked it.

❸ Yes, I think it would be a good idea to do that because there is so much pollution in cities and the car is responsible for a lot of that pollution. I'd be happy to walk or use a bicycle, anyway.

ROSYATI

❶ Nowhere! I'm much too busy for romantic holidays.

❷ I'd just sit and relax. I wouldn't try to escape, because sooner or later someone would unlock the door with a key, of course.

❸ I think that we have no alternative. The car is killing our cities. It is perhaps possible to develop fuel that is not poisonous like petrol is, but the car has changed the whole idea of a city from a friendly and interesting place for people to a sea of motorised madness. Yes, it would be a good idea to make the city centres peaceful again.

What were the three questions? Tick the boxes.

QUESTION 1

☐ a. Would a romantic holiday be enjoyable?

☐ b. Where would you go for a romantic holiday?

☐ c. Would Tahiti be the ideal place for a romantic holiday?

QUESTION 2

☐ a. How would you escape from a locked room?

☐ b. What would you do in an empty room?

☐ c. How would you open a closed door?

QUESTION 3

☐ a. Would it be impossible to ban cars from cities?

☐ b. Would it be a good idea to ban all cars from city centres?

☐ c. Would you stop noisy cars from entering cities?

---

6 I wouldn't like to be a man because …

8 What would you do?

Write the three questions from Exercise 7 and then your answers to them. Write short paragraphs.

Question 1: ....?

My answer: ....

....

Question 2: ....?

My answer: ....

....

Question 3: ....?

My answer: ....

....

9 Visual dictionary

Complete the visual dictionary for Unit 19 on page 141.

10 Reflections

Your English is improving. Think again about the things you would most like to do with your English. Put these possibilities in order of preference for you (put 1 for the most important, 2, 3 and so on). Add others of your own.

> I would most like to use my English:
> – to speak to people when I travel in an English-speaking country. ☐
> – to improve my career chances. ☐
> – to listen to music, and understand films from English-speaking countries. ☐
> – to study in an English-speaking country. ☐
> – to communicate better with English friends. ☐
> – to read newspapers, books and magazines from English-speaking countries. ☐
> – to write business letters and personal letters. ☐
> – to .... ☐
> – to .... ☐
> – to .... ☐

What are *you* doing to help your most important preferences?

I'm ....

....

20

I'M SO SORRY!

1 I'm ever so sorry!

polite complaints and replies in shops

A Look at the examples. A person complaining like the man on the left isn't very polite, and the reply isn't very polite either.

This watch is broken! Replace it!

I have to ask the manager.

Excuse me, this watch is broken. Can you replace it please?

Oh, I'm sorry, sir. Please wait a minute, I have to ask the manager about that.

Not polite

More polite

B Change the four complaints and the replies so that they are more polite. Use the expressions in the box if you like.

Customer	
Excuse me	madam (or sir)
Can you ...?	Could you ...?
I wonder if you could ... please?	
I'm afraid	Would you ...?

Shop assistant	
I apologise	Oh, I do apologise
I'm sorry	I'm very sorry (but)
I'm so sorry	I'm sorry about that
I'm ever so sorry (but)	
I'm terribly sorry	I'm really sorry
I'm afraid	

1. In a café
   CUSTOMER: This coffee's cold.
   WAITER: You can have another cup.

   CUSTOMER: ....

   WAITER: ....

2. In a shoe shop
   CUSTOMER: I bought these shoes last week. Look, the heel's already worn down.
   SHOP ASSISTANT: Where's your receipt?

   CUSTOMER: ....

   SHOP ASSISTANT: ....

3. At the bakery
   CUSTOMER: I asked for two loaves of bread. You've given me one.
   SHOP ASSISTANT: Here's the other one.

   CUSTOMER: ....

   SHOP ASSISTANT: ....

4. In an electrical shop
   CUSTOMER: This radio cassette doesn't work. Give me a refund.
   SHOP ASSISTANT: We don't give refunds.

   CUSTOMER: ....

   SHOP ASSISTANT: ....

📟 Listen to more polite versions of 1–4 and compare them with yours.

2 It's broken!
verb forms for describing complaints

Look at each picture. A shop assistant says to you *What's the matter with it?* Complete
the missing complaints.

	What's the matter with it? (short form)	*What is the matter with it?* (long form)
	a. It's stopped.	a. ....
	b.	b. It has got a crack.
	c.	c. It is dead.
	d. It's broken.	d. ....
	e.	e. There is a spider in the tin.
	f. It's lost one of its legs.	f. ....
	g. It doesn't work properly.	g. ....
	h. It's .... big.	h. ....
	i.	i. There is a button missing.
	j.	j. The ice cream has melted.

A Here are six situations. How would you say 'sorry' to the other person in each situation? Write your answers.

1. In a crowded bus, you step on someone's foot.

....

....

2. In a supermarket, you knock over some tins.

....

....

3. A friend invites you to a party. You forget to reply to the invitation. You ring up after the party to apologise and explain.

....

....

4. You arrange to meet someone. You arrive an hour late.

....

....

5. You open a letter. You see it's not for you, but for your friend.

....

....

6. You pick up another person's umbrella by mistake.

....

....

B 📼 Listen to six people apologising to someone in the same situations. Compare their apologies with yours.

4 At the shops

Match the shops on the left with the appropriate goods on the right.

Shops

1. jewellers
2. café
3. electrical shop
4. florist
5. video shop
6. health food shop
7. computer shop
8. chemist

Goods

a. antibiotic tablets
b. radio
c. ring
d. nuts
e. cappuccino
f. disk
g. roses
h. video tape

5 Well, do it yourself!

Read the sentences. Write /ɪ/, /e/ or /æ/ to show what you say to make the vowel sound in the last word. Is it /ɪ/ (b<u>i</u>t), /e/ (g<u>e</u>t) or /æ/ (gl<u>a</u>d)?

1. I've broken the <u>lid</u>. ......
2. He hasn't made the <u>bed</u>. ......
3. You've got the rug <u>wet</u>. ......
4. This glove doesn't <u>fit</u>. ......
5. There's a fly in the <u>tin</u>. ......
6. It's a quarter past <u>ten</u>! ......

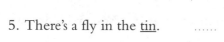
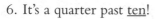

7. You didn't scrub the <u>pan</u>! ......
8. You didn't buy the <u>pen</u>! ......
9. You didn't drive the <u>van</u>! ......
10. You didn't pay the <u>men</u>! ......
11. You didn't clean my <u>hat</u>! ......
12. You didn't feed my <u>pet</u>! ......

Listen and check your answers. Then listen again and repeat each sentence.

6 I'm writing to apologise ...

A Read these three notes and answer the questions by ticking the appropriate box.

1. Which note has most language mistakes?   a. ☐   b. ☐   c. ☐
2. Which note is the most formal?   a. ☐   b. ☐   c. ☐
3. Which note is the best one to send to a close friend?   a. ☐   b. ☐   c. ☐
4. Which one is the best to write to your teacher?   a. ☐   b. ☐   c. ☐

> Dear Jim,
> I'm sorry i wasn't able to intend the Englsih classes last week, but I had very bad cold. I apologise for not leting you now. I hope to be back in class next week.
> Yours,
> Eddie

> Jim –
> Well, guess what? Yeah, I've got a really bad cold and couldn't make it to class. Typical isn't it? I never seem to be 100%. I should be back next week, OK? Sorry I didn't let you know before.
> Cheers,
> Lily

> Dear Mr Jones,
> I'm writing to apologise for not attending English classes last week. Unfortunately, I had a bad cold and forgot to inform you. I hope to rejoin the class next week.
> Yours sincerely,
> Masumi Nakamura

B Rewrite the letter that has the most mistakes. There are six changes to make.

A Read the following story about buying a car. Read quickly just to get an idea of the story.

I once bought a second-hand car from a used car dealer. It was in wonderful condition – one previous owner, bright paint, and not many miles on the clock. The car was a bit expensive but the dealer offered me a three months' guarantee. I was still a bit unsure so I asked the dealer to tell me the name of the previous owner. Then I phoned him up and asked lots of questions. Everything seemed OK, so I bought the car.

At first I was really pleased with the car and went on lots of long journeys – especially when it was hot, because it's best to drive a car a lot when there's only a short guarantee – then you can find out about other problems. In fact there were no problems. The car was fast, comfortable, quiet ... perfect. Then one day the car made terrible noises and stopped. It needed a new engine. I was angry and phoned the dealer to demand a new engine, but the dealer said he was sorry but the guarantee had finished because I'd bought the car exactly three months and one week before. I was furious but I couldn't do anything. A friend at work reminded me that the Romans had the expression 'Caveat emptor', which in Italian means 'Buyer be careful'. I said that in this case the Romans would say 'Car-veat emptor', or 'Buyer of car be careful'. He laughed, but I didn't find it very funny.

B 📼 Read while you listen to a person telling the same story. There are some differences. What are the two mistakes in the written story, and the three pieces of new information that you hear?

The two mistakes:

1. ....

2. ....

The three pieces of new information:

1. ....

2. ....

3. ....

Imagine that you bought the car in the story. Complete this letter to a consumer organisation complaining about what happened. Use some of the language in the story to help you.

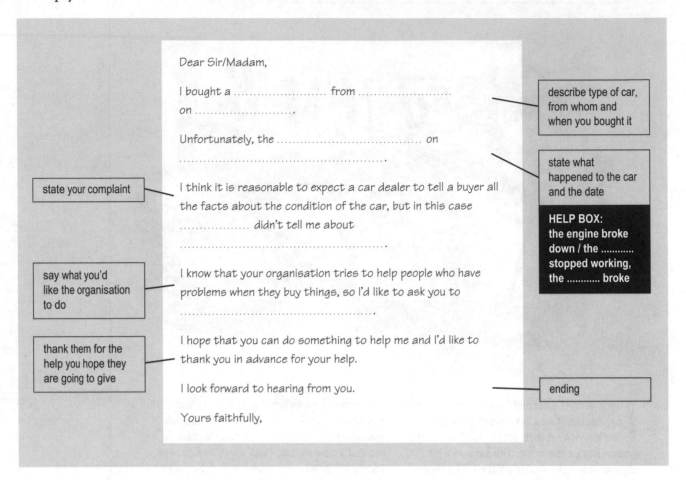

Dear Sir/Madam,

I bought a .... from ....
on ....

> describe type of car, from whom and when you bought it

Unfortunately, the .... on
....

> state what happened to the car and the date

> **HELP BOX:**
> the engine broke down / the .... stopped working, the .... broke

state your complaint

I think it is reasonable to expect a car dealer to tell a buyer all the facts about the condition of the car, but in this case .... didn't tell me about
....

say what you'd like the organisation to do

I know that your organisation tries to help people who have problems when they buy things, so I'd like to ask you to
....

thank them for the help you hope they are going to give

I hope that you can do something to help me and I'd like to thank you in advance for your help.

I look forward to hearing from you.

> ending

Yours faithfully,

9 Visual dictionary

Complete the visual dictionary for Unit 20 on page 142.

10 Reflections – cultural differences

Think of a time when you visited another country or visited some people from another culture. Make notes about one or two cultural differences.

....
....
....

....

When you try to complain or apologise in shops or in other situations, are there any differences between what happens in your country and what happens in other countries you have visited? Make notes.

....
....
....

21

ALL YOU NEED IS LOVE ... OR MONEY

1 I don't really need it but I want it!

need; want; would like

Complete the sentences by adding *need*, *want* or *would like* (*...'d like*) in the blanks. Use the appropriate form (positive, negative, present or past).

1. You don't .... to be mad to work here, but it helps!

2. I've always .... to see Africa, and now that I'm retired, I'm going to go.

3. She's terribly rich; she .... to save up her money, but she does anyway.

4. He's just not very good with money: he .... to save up some money, but somehow he never does.

5. They live very simply and don't .... very much money.

6. My computer has broken, so I .... a new one. I .... the biggest model but I don't think I've got enough money for that.

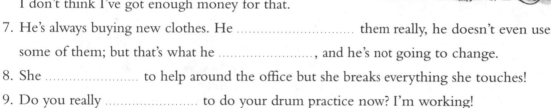

7. He's always buying new clothes. He .... them really, he doesn't even use some of them; but that's what he ...., and he's not going to change.

8. She .... to help around the office but she breaks everything she touches!

9. Do you really .... to do your drum practice now? I'm working!

10. Well, you told me to practise! Do you .... me to get that job with the pop group, or not?

2 All you need

need (to)

Which of these sentences need *to*? Add *to* in the blank, if it is necessary.

1. All you need is .... love, love, love. That's what the song says.

2. But I need .... have a bit of money too.

3. I'd like .... a lot of money, actually.

4. No, not really. You want .... earn enough, that's all.

5. She's always wanted .... a dog.

6. Well, he'd like .... get a cat, he doesn't want .... look after a dog.

7. Maybe they need .... buy some goldfish.

8. They've got a lovely little house, but they'd like .... move to a luxury flat.

9. That's silly. They need .... something to keep them busy, that's what they need.

3 Money, money, money

Match the countries with their currencies.

| France   Germany   Brazil |
| Japan   England |
| Eire (the Republic of Ireland) |
| Spain   Italy   the USA |
| Indonesia   Russia |
| Sweden   China |

| franc   yuan |
| Deutschmark   yen |
| kronor   pound sterling |
| real   punt |
| peseta   lira   dollar |
| rouble   rupiah |

4 We want to get rich ... quickly!

A All of these adjectives can go with one of the two verbs. Which verb? Tick the box.

Adjectives
happy   rich   good   worried   safe   better   worse

Verbs
to get ☐   to feel ☐

B Which adjectives usually go with the other verb?

....

C Which other words go with these? Make nine new expressions using the words in the box.

Example: *stock exchange*

stock	....	....	
standard of	....		
long-distance	....	....	
high	....	....	
bank	....	....	

price	manager
living	exchange
salary	call
broker	account
flight	

5 What do you need to be happy?

A Answer the question by making a list of things in each column.

To be happy you need	*To be happy you don't need*
....	....
....	....
....	....
....	....
....	....
....	....

B ⬚ Listen to two people answering the question. Tick the things on your lists that they also mention. Add the things they say that aren't on your list.

A Answer these questions.

What job did (or do) your parents want you to have?   ....

What job did (or do) your friends think you should have?   ....

B Read this text. It's from a book about how to be successful. Follow the instructions in the text.

Exercise 1:   DO IT FOR YOU.

This exercise helps you to know you ... what you really want ... what you really enjoy ... what really interests you.

Sit down with a pencil and some paper. At the top of the first sheet of paper, put:

Step One

WHAT MY PARENTS WANTED (OR WANT) ME TO BE:

Write down the career your parents chose for you. For example, if your parents wanted you to get married and have a family, write down:

WHAT MY PARENTS WANTED ME TO BE: A HOMEMAKER

If your parents really wanted you to follow in your dad's footsteps and take over the business, write down:

WHAT MY PARENTS WANTED ME TO BE: A BUSINESSPERSON

Then make a list of the things that your parents valued – in detail. What did they say were good qualities for a homemaker or businessperson to have?

Step Two

Take another sheet of paper and begin a second list. Write at the top:

WHAT MY FRIENDS THINK I SHOULD BE:
(for example: nurse, artist, restaurant owner ...)

What do your friends think are important qualities for this career? Again, list as many things as you can think of.

Step Three

Make a third list, headed:

I DON'T WANT TO BE A ....

Add as many things as you can. Write down all the things you would hate to be.

Step Four

Begin a fourth list:

PROBABLY I'D LIKE TO BE A ....

Don't worry about making a mistake. This is not decision time. You are just practising new ways of thinking and acting. Write down anything that you find interesting. Write down everything, even things that seem impossible ... just for practice.

When you are all finished, take the first three lists, 'What my parents wanted me to be', 'What my friends think I should be', and 'I don't want to be a ...' and

THROW THEM AWAY.

Keep only the last list, 'Probably I'd like to be a ...'. It shows your own feelings. This is just a beginning. But you can use it to begin building on more positive action.

C Are the following statements similar to (*S*) or different from (*D*) what the text says?

1. The exercise helps you to understand yourself better. ☐
2. Step 1 tells you about the values of your parents. ☐
3. Step 2 tells you how your friends see their jobs. ☐
4. Step 3 tells you what you really like. ☐
5. Step 4 tells you what you think you can do. ☐
6. Step 4 is the time to decide on your career. ☐
7. The only important list for you is list 4. ☐

7 You need to pass your secondary school exams   writing

Read the three questions.

In your country:

What do you need to do to open a bank account?
What do you need to do to buy a house?
What do you need to do to enter university?

Choose one of the questions. Write a short paragraph to tell English-speaking people what you need to do in your country.

Example: *In my country, to … the first thing you need to do is to …*
You also need to … and to …
Another thing you need to do is to …
Finally, you need to …

8 Visual dictionary

Complete the visual dictionary for Unit 21 on page 143.

9 Reflections: a learning curve   thinking about language learning

Learning curve 1

Learning curve 2

You read a text from a book about success in Exercise 6. These are two 'learning curves' from the same book.

Do you think your 'learning curve' for English is like number 1 or number 2?

....

Which do you think is a successful curve? Can you give reasons?

....

Which do you think is a successful curve?

....

22

THE RIGHT CLIMATE?

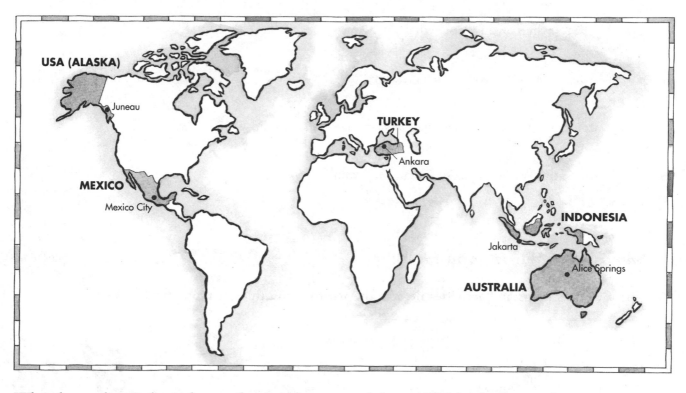

What do you know about the weather in other parts of the world? Match the questions and answers.

1. What's it like in Ankara, Turkey?
2. What's it like in Jakarta, Indonesia?
3. What's it like in Alice Springs, Australia?
4. What's it like in Juneau, Alaska?
5. What's it like in Mexico City, Mexico?

Answers:

a. It's hot all year round and very dry.
b. It's quite a wet climate, really. It rains almost every day in the spring and autumn. The summers are beautiful but very short. In the winter, there's snow, but it can be mild and often wet.
c. It's very hot in the summer, and dry. The winters are cold, with quite a lot of snow and ice.
d. It's lovely all year round. It's quite a mild climate and the temperature doesn't change much – but sometimes the summers get very hot. The mornings are usually fine, there's a bit of rain in the middle of the day, then the afternoons are sunny again.
e. It's hot and humid all year round. There are no real seasons.

2 What's the weather like in your country? writing about the weather

A Write a brief description of the weather in the part of your country where you live.

In .... there are .... seasons. In .... it's ....,
but in .... it's usually .... Sometimes it can be
.... The best time of year is ....; the worst time is probably
in .... because it is ....

B Unscramble the questions, check your answers (page 173), then give your own answers to the questions.

Question

1. Q: seasons you have many how do ? ....
   A: ....

2. Q: in average July is what the temperature ? ....
   A: ....

3. Q: is it hot when you do what do very ? ....
   A: ....

4. Q: if is there a do you what storm do ? ....
   A: ....

5. Q: you do go where a national when is there holiday ? ....
   A: ....

6. Q: like in summer it what's town in your ? ....
   A: ....

3 Snowy weather is good for skiing

A Write clothes items and activities next to the weather you think is most suitable for them.

Clothes	Weather	Activities
....	freezing	....
....	snowy	....
....	cold	....
....	chilly	....
....	cool	....
....	sunny and boiling hot	....
....	wet	

a swimsuit

reading

tennis

a heavy overcoat

a sunhat

a jacket

a pullover

walking

golf

an umbrella

sailing

skiing

swimming

shorts

a scarf

gloves

a T-shirt

sunbathing

B Complete the sentences. Use expressions from Part A.

1. When it's hot and sunny outside, make sure you put on ....

2. When it's freezing outside, remember to wear ....

3. Remember not to sit too long in the sun when it's ....

4. Don't forget your umbrella when it's ....

5. When the evenings are chilly, wear ....

4 What do you do when it's hot?
pronunciation: stress and rhythm in questions

A 🔲 Listen to the instructions and repeat.

Write down Questions 1 and 2 and mark the syllables which have the main stress.

Question 1 ....?

Question 2 ....?

B 🔲 Listen to the instructions. Ask Questions 1 and 2, listen to the replies and write them down.

Reply to Question 1 ....

Reply to Question 2 ....

5 What do you do when you don't know a word?
listening: *if* and *when* clauses

A Here are some answers. Write appropriate questions. Use *if* or *when* in your questions.

Example: *I drink a lot and sleep a lot.*
 Possible question: *What do you do when the weather's very hot?*

1. Q: ....?

 A: I lie awake at night.

2. Q: ....?

 A: I look it up in the dictionary.

3. Q: ....?

 A: I just relax.

4. Q: ....?

 A: I make myself a cup of tea.

5. Q: ....?

 A: I phone up my friend for a chat.

B 🔲 Listen to two people doing the same task. Write down their questions and compare them with yours.

1. Q: ....?

2. Q: ....?

3. Q: ....?

4. Q: ....?

5. Q: ....?

A Read these sentences. What are they about?

It is the human body's largest single organ.
Can you guess? If you can, give yourself 3 marks.
If not, read on:
It weighs 4 kilos and measures about 2 square metres.
Can you guess? If you can, give yourself 2 marks.
If not, read on:
If something destroys more than a quarter of it, the body cannot survive.
Can you guess? If you can, give yourself a pat on the back!

Read the text and see if your guesses are right.

It is the human body's largest single organ. It weighs 4 kilos and measures about 2 square metres. If more than a quarter of it is destroyed by burns, the body cannot survive. It is called the skin.

It is waterproof, airproof and can repair itself. But as we get older, it is not able to give the same protection. People with blue, green or hazel eyes and fair skin have a higher risk of developing skin cancer.

A Plan for Prevention

Here's how to prevent skin damage caused by the sun.

▌ **USE** sunblock cream. Put it on fifteen minutes before you go out into the sun.

▌ **WEAR** a hat and close-weave fabrics. Wear a shirt with a collar, not a T-shirt (remember, a wet T-shirt still transmits UV radiation).

▌ **TRY TO WORK** or play outdoors before 11 am and after 3 pm to avoid the very dangerous times of the day for sun burn.

Some people now use sunblock 365 days a year, and it is now put into some make-up products. Anti-cancer groups say that young people are difficult to educate about protection of skin from the sun. In the 30+ age group, however, people are now really aware of the dangers.

B Add expressions from the text to fill these spaces.

skin: waterproof; ....

clothes for skin protection: hat; ....

products for skin protection: some make-up; ....

C Are these statements true or false, according to the text? Write *T* or *F* in the boxes.

1. Air can pass through skin. ☐
2. Water can pass through skin. ☐
3. People with blue, green or hazel eyes and fair skin are more likely to get skin cancer. ☐
4. The skin gives less protection to older people. ☐
5. A wet T-shirt gives good protection from the sun. ☐
6. Young people are less interested than older people in learning about skin protection. ☐
7. All make-up products now have sun protection. ☐

7 Leave a note

7 Leave a note

A Sometimes friends or family come to stay in your flat or house for the first time. If you are at work or out of the house, you can leave notes to help them. Think of your house or flat and then complete the notes. Add two new notes.

If you go out, ...   When you leave, ...

If you want to cook a meal, ...   If you want to phone overseas, ...

If you use the car, ...   If you go into the city, ...

If there are any phone calls, ...   If you need to contact me, ...

If you want to use the phone, ...

B Are any of the notes about things that annoy you when people come to stay?

Write one or two sentences about things that annoy you about guests.

Example: *I get really annoyed when guests forget to pay for their international phone calls.*

....

....

8 A DIY poem

Here is a poem about relationships. Choose suitable words to complete the poem. Show your poem to your teacher, if you like.

When I arrive, she (or he) goes.   If I laugh, she (he) ....

When I get up, she (or he) ....   When I'm ...., she (he) says

When I'm ...., she's (or he's) ....   Why are we so .... these days?

When I want to go out, she (he) wants to ....

9 Visual dictionary

Complete the visual dictionary for Unit 22 on page 144.

10 Reflections

In some English-speaking countries, the weather is used as a comfortable topic of polite conversation.

How important is the weather in your culture? Do people talk about it much? Can you remember any hurricanes, floods or other natural disasters? Have they become part of your country's literature, music or art?

Write a few sentences.

Examples: *In my culture, the weather is ...*
            In .... there was a bad ...
            In .... there is a book about ...

....

....

....

....

23

FESTIVALS

Put these sentences into the appropriate boxes.

I'd love to, but I'm afraid I can't.
Would you like to come to our house on Saturday?
Yes, I'd love to. Thanks for asking me.
I've got to go to work on Saturday.

INVITING

ACCEPTING

DECLINING POLITELY

REASON

📼 Listen to check your dialogue.

📼 Listen. Write in the missing parts of these mini-dialogues.

1. A: Would you like to come to my birthday party on Friday?

   B: ....

2. A: .... ?

   B: I can't, I'm afraid, my parents are having a wedding anniversary party.

3. A: Can you come for a coffee this morning?

   B: ....

4. A: Would you like to come out for lunch?

   B: ....

📼 Now listen to the invitations and accept or refuse after each one.

3 Shall I help you with the washing up?

offering with *shall*; accepting; declining

Put the numbers of the correct speech balloons into the cartoons.

1. *Shall I carry that for you, sir?*

2. *Shall we go out to eat tonight?*

3. *Yes, please. I want to finish this book.*

4. *Oh, yes, thank you. It's very heavy.*

5. *No, it's OK. I'll do it.*

6. *Shall I help you with the washing up?*

7. *Shall I take the dog for a walk?*

8. *Good idea, there's nothing in here.*

Listen to the mini conversations. Check your answers.

4 Word friends

vocabulary

Which of these expressions are often used after *birthday*? after *happy*?

1. birthday

| party | festival | road | cake | card | pencil |

birthday ....; birthday ....; birthday ....

2. Happy

| New Year | Morning | Easter | Today | Birthday | Anniversary |

Happy ....; Happy ....; Happy ....; Happy ....

5 I have a special thing that I do on my birthday

listening

A Listen to three people talking. Which of the expressions in the box do the speakers mention?

Speaker 1

....

....

Speaker 2

....

....

Speaker 3

....

....

a bunch of flowers
Easter   birthday
chocolate eggs
coffee and cake
Friday nights

B Complete these sentences.

1. On her own b................., Speaker 1 sends flowers to her ....

2. Speaker 2's parents hide .... in the .... at Easter time.

3. Speaker 3 has .... brothers and they always clear up after the family meal on Fridays.

Then the sons .... their parents.

6 Festival of tomatoes

A Write the names of two important festivals in your country or city.

....

Is either of them a new festival?   Yes/No

B Look at the pictures. Quickly read the text about traditional and modern festivals in Spain. Which pictures are of festivals in the text?

La Tomatina

SPAIN is a country full of music, colour and energy. It is not surprising that festivals, or fiestas, are important. There are more than 3000 in modern Spain. Of course traditional festivals are well known, those at Easter for example, and many people outside Spain have seen pictures of bulls running in the streets of Pamplona and, more recently, in the suburban streets of Madrid. But how many visitors to Spain have heard of the fiesta in Castillo de Murcia, Burgos? Here an athletic man called a *calocho* or naughty devil jumps over several sick babies lying on mattresses to try to help them to get better.

Not many visitors to Spain have seen a new fiesta called *La Tomatina*. *La Tomatina* takes place in a village called Bunyols in Valencia. During *La Tomatina*, villagers throw 70,000 kilos of very ripe tomatoes at each other for fifteen minutes. Visitors can join in too. The fiesta started after a lorry accidentally spilt its load of tomatoes in the village square. It has become popular, more popular than the cleaning up the following week, when villagers have to whitewash their buildings!

C Read the text again. Are these statements true or false? Write *T* or *F* in the boxes.

1. There are over 3000 festivals in modern Spain. ☐
2. Bull-running takes place in more than one part of Spain. ☐
3. The babies on the mattress in Castillo de Murcia are not sick. ☐
4. The tomatoes for the fiesta in Bunyols are not yet ripe. ☐
5. Tourists in Bunyols can throw tomatoes too. ☐
6. After *La Tomatina*, villagers have to clean the buildings. ☐

7 Would you like to come?

writing

A Read the invitation card.

We are having a surprise birthday party for Mario on Saturday, 5th July at 9.30 pm. Would you like to come?

The party is going to be at 5 Via Sole, Firenze.

Please let me know if you can come.

Yours,
Luigi

B Write a reply to the party invitation. Decline the invitation. Be polite and give a reason.

Dear Luigi,

Thanks for your i...........................
....
....

C Write down the names and birthday dates of two people you know well.

Name	Birthday
....	....
....	....

D On the two other invitation cards, write notes inviting someone to your friends' birthday parties on the dates on your list. Show your teacher, if you like.

8 Visual dictionary

Complete the visual dictionary for Unit 23 on page 145.

9 Reflections

A Write down simple ways of inviting, accepting and declining politely in your own language for some of the situations in this unit.

inviting ....

accepting ....

declining politely ....

B Compare them with English. Which of these seems to be true? Tick the boxes.

My first language seems:

more direct ☐   less direct ☐
more polite ☐   less polite ☐
In my language we   give reasons ☐   don't give reasons ☐   when we refuse an invitation politely.
In my language we use more words than in English to thank people for their invitations. ☐

C Write down a few comments about any cultural differences you discovered in this unit.

Example: *In my country, we don't usually have birthday parties and we don't write invitation cards.*

In my country, we ....

....

....

LOOKING AHEAD

Write the underlined time expressions under *Past* or *Future*.

I'll be 35 <u>later this year</u>.
Life was hard <u>at that time</u>.
I'll be back <u>soon</u>.
I'm going to Fiji <u>next year</u>.
Children needed to study hard <u>then</u>.
<u>Five years from now</u>, all children will need
   to have computers.
See you <u>in a minute</u>!
I was unemployed a year <u>ago</u>.

Past	*Future*
....	*later this year*
....	....
....	....
....	....
....	....

A Now the year is ....
In ten years from now the year will be ....

Write the name of someone you know in each of these spaces.

Example: <u>*Jim*</u> *will be over 50 in ten years from now.*

1. .... will be over 50 in ten years from now.

2. .... will be over 70 in ten years from now.

3. .... will be between 30 and 40 in ten years from now.

4. I'll be .... in ten years ....

5. .... will be .... next year.

B Complete the sentences with an appropriate word.

6. My country will be (more) .... (er) in ten years from now.

7. My city will be .... in ten years from now.

8. People will eat more .... in ten years from now.

Answer these questions about yourself and your country. Write either *Yes, I will / Yes, they will / Yes, it won't* or *No, I won't / No, they won't / No, it won't*.

Examples: Will all children need to know about computers in ten years from now?
Yes, they will.
Will you have an important job in two years' time?
No, I won't.
Will your country still have a traffic problem in ten years' time?
Yes, it will.

1. Q: Will your country have really serious traffic problems in fifteen years from now?

   A: ....

2. Q: Will your country have a new prime minister in ten years from now?

   A: ....

3. Q: Will you have more leisure time when you are old?

   A: ....

4. Q: Will your country have more tourism in ten years from now?

   A: ....

5. Q: Will children need to study harder in the future?

   A: ....

6. Q: In ten years' time, will your country be a better place to live in?

   A: ....

7. Q: Will your English be excellent in ten years' time?

   A: ....

We asked some people the same questions. Write down the answers they gave. Check them in the tapescript on page 159.

1. ....
2. ....
3. ....
4. ....
5. ....
6. ....
7. ....

Read these examples.

She's going to have her baby next month. (Her <u>present</u> condition has decided what is going to happen in the future.)
I can't go on your boat, I'll be sick. (I'm predicting what will happen in that situation.)
The door bell rings, I say to my friend inside the house 'I'll go.' (I'm talking about a decision at the same time as making the decision.)

Complete these sentences with *going to* (+ the correct form of the verb *to be*) or *will*.

1. I'm so tired, I .... sleep right now!

2. It's OK, you sit there and rest, I .... answer the phone!

3. He's sold his house and he .... live in Canada.

4. I'd love more ice cream, but I'm so full, I .... be ill, so no, thanks.

6 Russian electricians

pronunciation: /l/ and /r/

Rewrite these sentences so that they make sense.

1. regularly electricians I'll long lonely write to Russian letters

....

2. your rapidly They'll letters read correct long errors spelling and the

....

⊂⊃ Now listen and repeat the words you hear after the question.

Example: 1. *What will you do?*
            (you hear) *I'll* (you repeat *I'll*)
            (you hear) *I'll write* (you repeat *I'll write*)

7 Will people still write letters in ten years' time?

listening

Two women (Lyn and Kate) and two men (Tris and Ian) are talking about the future.

⊂⊃ Read the four questions they ask, then listen and write *1* next to the first question you hear, *2* next to the second question you hear, and so on. Change any of the notes that are not correct.

Question number		Notes – are they correct?
☐	Will children study at home and not at school?	Ian doesn't think so. Tris says school helps children to learn social skills.
☐	Will people still use cash?	Tris says yes they will, more and more, especially in the United States.
☐	Will people still write letters?	Kate says yes.
☐	Will city life become more pleasant?	Lyn says it will be better.

8 Will it be one or two?

reading and writing

A ▤ Put each of the words in the box in the appropriate column.

One person	*Two people*	
....	....	alone couple pair single individual
....	....	divorced married partners
....	....	
....	....	

B This text is about being single and being a couple in countries like the US and the UK. What do you think it will say? Choose two of the following possibilities.

a. It will say that single people are often unhappy.
b. It will say that married people are unhappy.
c. It will say that more and more people in countries like the US and UK are choosing not to get married or have a partner.
d. It will say that single people enjoy their freedom.

Read the text and see if you are right.

More and more women and men believe that it is now possible to live happily as single people, not as couples. There is still social pressure to marry and become a couple, but statistics show that people are becoming less happy with the idea of being in a team of two.

Research shows that many divorced people are happier and healthier on their own. More women between thirty and forty in the UK and USA are choosing to stay single. Even the number of divorces among people over 65 is increasing.

People who are single and happy consider themselves complete human beings. They don't believe they need a partner to become complete. As one single woman says, 'I find it insulting to think that the only way I shall find happiness is by spending my life with another person. I'm extremely happy on my own, thanks very much, and no, I don't get lonely. I think we need to stop celebrating engagements, weddings and wedding anniversaries, and consider those women and men who choose to live on their own. Single people can really have love, career, money and a happy, active social life without the problem of a permanent partner. They can develop as individuals and have their own space. I will never get married. It's great to have freedom – freedom, for example, to change all the furniture in your flat in the middle of the night.'

But the fact is that there is still a lot of social pressure to become a couple. Will this change in the future? Will women in many societies find marriage less attractive as their freedom grows? Do single people really have the key to happiness? Another single woman seems to believe so. She says, 'There's such a sense of freedom in feeling that you don't have to look for a partner, in realising that a partner is not necessary for happiness.'

C Match the two halves of these sentences about the text.

1. You don't need to be married
2. Marriage
3. Single people can have a full life

a. is still a social expectation.
b. without a partner.
c. to be a whole person.

D Write three sentences about the text. Say what you think about it.

Examples: 1. I think the text is *right* because *many single people are happy.*
2. In some ways I agree with the text. I think people in the future will *marry less and single people will be happier than many married people.*
3. In other ways I disagree with the text. In my society most people will *continue to marry, have children and have a happy life.*

1. I think the text is .... because ....

2. In some ways I agree with the text. I think people in the future will

....

3. In other ways I disagree with the text. In my society most people will

....

Write notes to leave for friends. Tell them where you are going, when you'll be back, when you'll see them. Apologise for not being able to join them for the activity you organised.

Example:

I'm going to work. I'll be back about 11. I'll see you in the morning. Sorry I won't be able to join you for the meal.

Jim

10 Visual dictionary

Complete the visual dictionary for Unit 24 on page 146.

11 Reflections for the future

This is the final unit in your Personal Study Workbook. Think about your studies in the future. Read these sentences and complete the ones that are appropriate to you.

1. Things you plan (or even promise!) to do to improve your English:

I'll start to read ....

I'll read more ....

I'll listen to ....

I'll listen to .... more often.

I'll speak English in ....

I'll speak English with ....

I'll speak English ....

I'll write in English to ....

2. About how long will it take you to:

   – reach the standard of spoken English you think you need? ....

   – reach the standard of written English you think you need? ....

3. How much time will you study in a class / on your own each week?

   I'll try to study for about .... hours per day / per week in a class, and about ....

   hours on my own per day / per week.

4. What will you need to do to learn faster and more effectively?

   I'll need to ....

   ....

   ....

   ....

Good luck with your English in the future.

VISUAL DICTIONARY

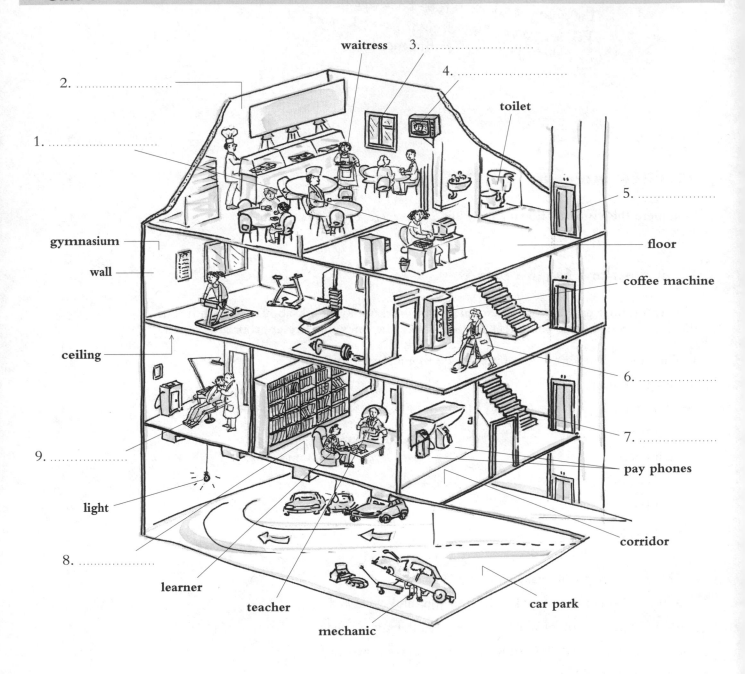

waitress
3. ....
4. ....
toilet
2. ....
1. ....
5. ....

gymnasium
wall
floor
coffee machine

ceiling
6. ....

7. ....
pay phones

9. ....

light
corridor

8. ....
learner
teacher
car park
mechanic

| stairs | library | cafeteria | television | dentist | lift | window | secretary | cleaner |

MORE NEW WORDS

....
....
....
....

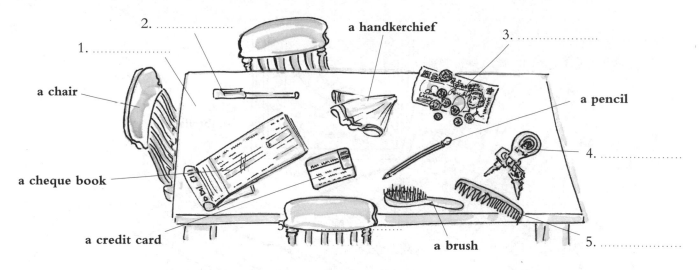

1. ....
2. ....
a handkerchief
3. ....
a chair
a pencil
4. ....
a cheque book
a credit card
a brush
5. ....

MORE NEW WORDS

| a pen |
| a table |
| car keys |
| a comb |
| money |

....
....
....
....

oranges
9. ....
apples
1. ....
beef
6. ....
croissants
bread
beans
peppers
prawns
fruit juice
onions
lamb
cake
rice
potatoes
2. ....
tuna
10. ....
3. ....
cucumber
7. ....
mineral water
11. ....
4. ....
8. ....
cheese
5. ....
12. ....

MORE NEW WORDS

milk	lettuce
carrots	bread rolls
bananas	chicken
pineapple	ice cream
grapes	noodles
salmon	sardines

....
....
....
....
....
....

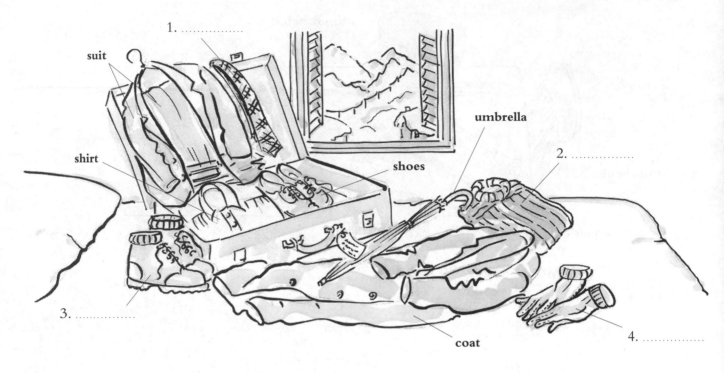

1. ....

suit

shirt

umbrella

shoes

2. ....

3. ....

4. ....

coat

5. ....

sun hat

jacket

jeans

dress

6. ....

sunglasses

7. ....

swimsuit

8. ....

| tie | T-shirt | shorts | skirt | gloves | sweater | boots | sandals |

MORE NEW WORDS

....
....
....
....

VISUAL DICTIONARY

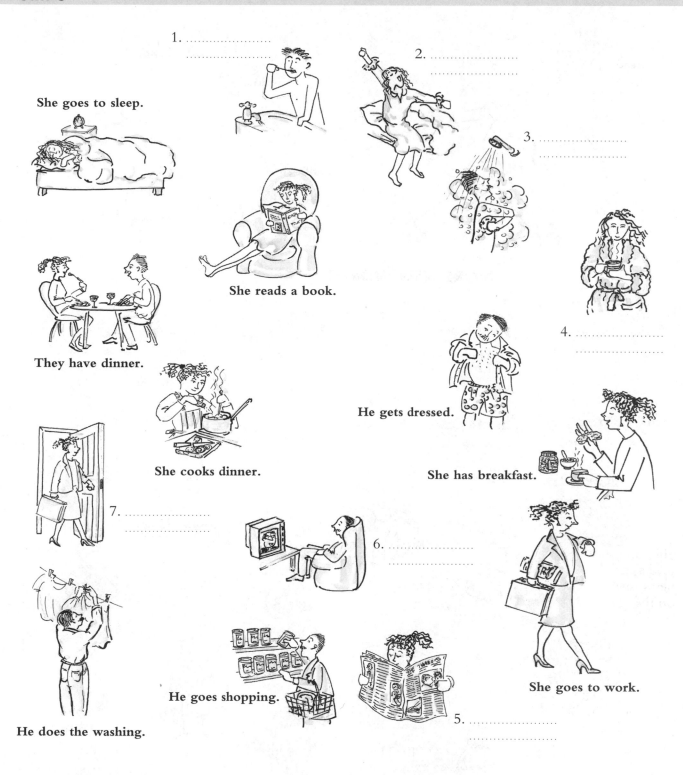

She goes to sleep.

1. ....
....

2. ....
....

3. ....
....

She reads a book.

They have dinner.

She cooks dinner.

He gets dressed.

4. ....
....

She has breakfast.

7. ....
....

6. ....
....

She goes to work.

He does the washing.

He goes shopping.

5. ....
....

| He watches television. | He cleans his teeth. | She comes home. | He has a shower. |
| She reads the paper. | She gets up. | She has a cup of coffee. | |

MORE NEW WORDS

....
....
....
....

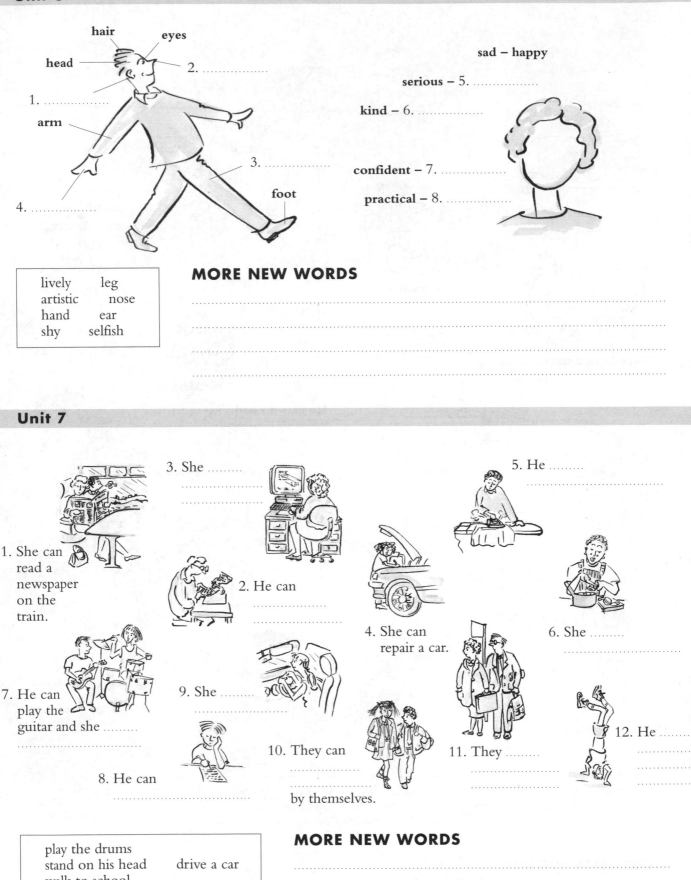

hair   eyes

head   2. ....

1. ....

arm

3. ....

4. ....   foot

sad – happy

serious – 5. ....

kind – 6. ....

confident – 7. ....

practical – 8. ....

lively	leg
artistic	nose
hand	ear
shy	selfish

MORE NEW WORDS

....

....

....

....

Unit 7

1. She can read a newspaper on the train.

3. She ....
....
....

5. He ....
....

2. He can
....

4. She can repair a car.

6. She ....
....

7. He can play the guitar and she ....
....

9. She ....

8. He can
....

10. They can
....
by themselves.

11. They ....
....

12. He ....
....

play the drums	
stand on his head	drive a car
walk to school	
use a computer	iron clothes
type	write a letter
go to work by bus	
cook dinner	

MORE NEW WORDS

....

....

....

....

....

VISUAL DICTIONARY

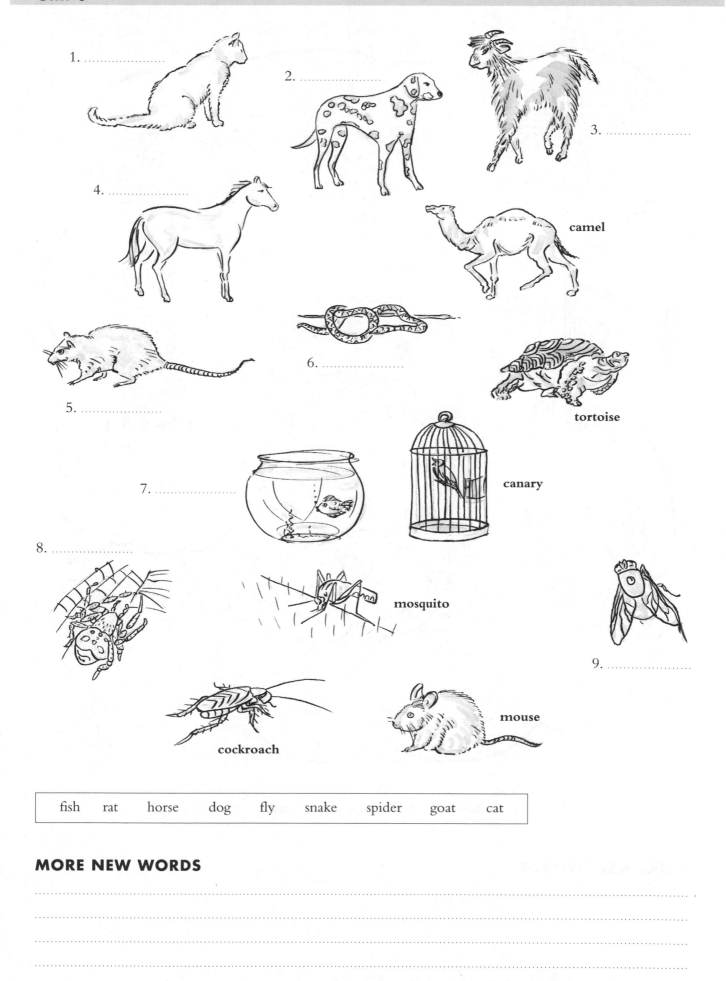

1. ....

2. ....

3. ....

camel

4. ....

5. ....

6. ....

tortoise

7. ....

canary

8. ....

mosquito

9. ....

cockroach

mouse

| fish | rat | horse | dog | fly | snake | spider | goat | cat |

MORE NEW WORDS

....

....

....

....

1. I .... in a big city.

2. We .... in that city until I was fifteen years old.

3. I .... to school every day.

4. I .... at school at eight in the morning.

5. My headteacher's name .... Mrs Billow.

6. I .... English and maths.

7. I .... very good at maths.

8. I .... with my friends in the streets after school.

| arrived | lived | was | went | was | played | stayed | liked |

MORE NEW WORDS

....

....

....

....

1. They .... in a café.

2. She spoke to him first.

3. She ...., 'Can you pass the salt, please?

4. They began to talk.

5. They .... a meal together.

6. They went to the cinema.

7. She bought a box of chocolates.

8. They .... a sad film.

9. They .... back to the café.

10. They had a cup of tea.

11. They .... for a long time.

12. He .... her about his wife and children.

13. She stood up in a fury.

14. A shot .... out.

15. She .... out of the café.

16. She .... a bus and disappeared.

17. He did not die, but he never forgot her.

| rang | saw | met | went | ran | said | told | caught | sat | ate |

MORE NEW WORDS

....

....

....

....

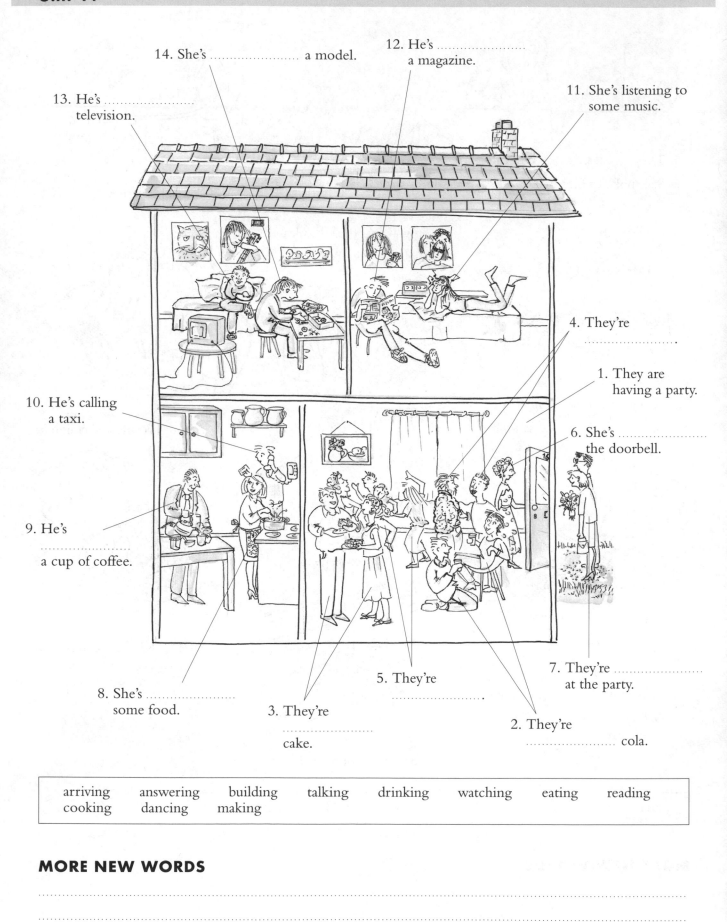

14. She's .... a model.

12. He's ....
a magazine.

11. She's listening to
some music.

13. He's ....
television.

4. They're
....

1. They are
having a party.

10. He's calling
a taxi.

6. She's ....
the doorbell.

9. He's
....
a cup of coffee.

7. They're ....
at the party.

8. She's ....
some food.

5. They're
....

3. They're
....
cake.

2. They're
.... cola.

| arriving | answering | building | talking | drinking | watching | eating | reading |
| cooking | dancing | making | | | | | |

MORE NEW WORDS

....

....

....

....

1. In January, I'm going to visit my brother in Jamaica.

2. In February, I'm going to ....

3. In March, I'm going to ....

4. In April, I'm ....

5. In May, I'm ....

6. In June, I'm ....

7. In July, I'm going to ....

8. In August, I'm going to ....

9. In September, ...

10. In October, we're going ....

11. In November, we're ....

12. In December, ...

---

going to do some gardening   move to a new town   I'm going to get married
going to buy a new car   have a birthday party   going to paint the kitchen
learn to drive a car   to visit my parents   going to change my job   we're going to go skiing
go on holiday by the sea

MORE NEW WORDS

....
....
....
....

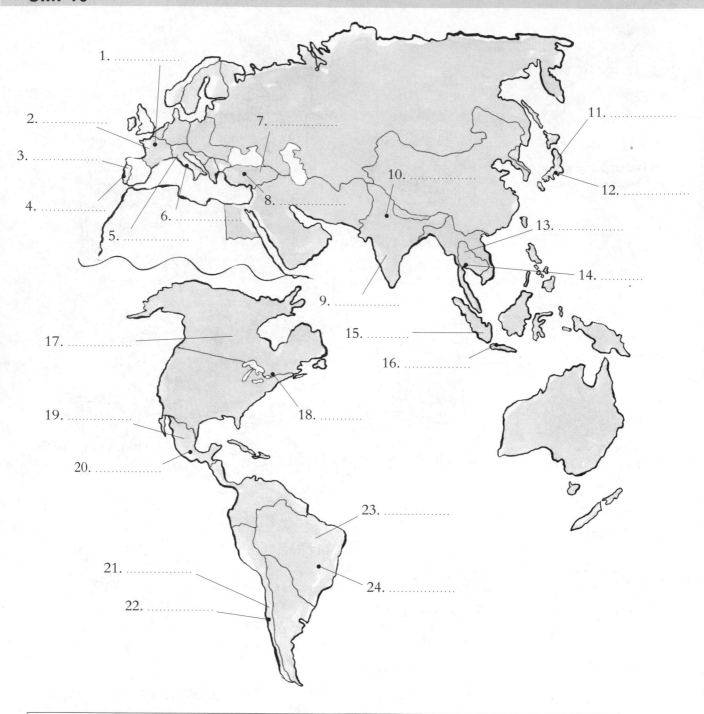

1. ....
2. ....
3. ....
4. ....
5. ....
6. ....
7. ....
8. ....
9. ....
10. ....
11. ....
12. ....
13. ....
14. ....
15. ....
16. ....
17. ....
18. ....
19. ....
20. ....
21. ....
22. ....
23. ....
24. ....

| Indonesia | Turkey | Canada | India | Mexico | Thailand | Chile | Japan |
| France | Portugal | Brazil | Italy | | | | |

| Paris | Tokyo | Rome | Ankara | Mexico City | Bangkok | Lisbon | Brasilia |
| Ottawa | New Delhi | Santiago | Jakarta | | | | |

MORE NEW WORDS

....
....
....
....

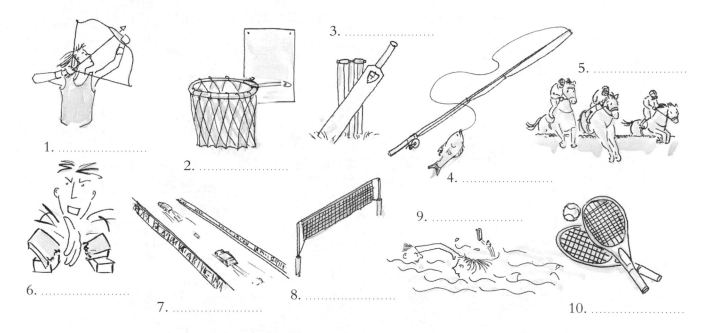

1. ....
2. ....
3. ....
4. ....
5. ....
6. ....
7. ....
8. ....
9. ....
10. ....

fishing	motor racing
karate	volleyball
tennis	swimming
cricket	archery
basketball	horse racing

MORE NEW WORDS

....
....
....
....

1. ....
2. ....
3. ....
4. ....
5. ....
6. ....
7. ....
8. ....
9. ....
10. ....
11. ....
12. ....
13. ....
14. ....
15. ....

desk	bin	letters	envelopes
filing cabinet	in-tray		
telephone	disk	computer	
calculator	facsimile machine		
keyboard	office chair	calendar	
photocopier			

MORE NEW WORDS

....
....
....
....
....

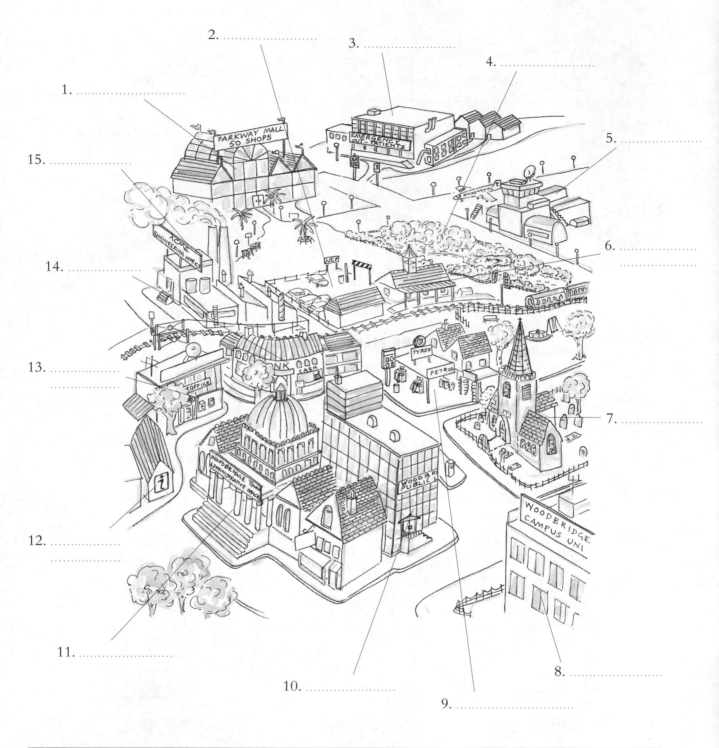

1. ....
2. ....
3. ....
4. ....
5. ....
6. ....
7. ....
8. ....
9. ....
10. ....
11. ....
12. ....
13. ....
14. ....
15. ....

| church | car park | airport | hospital | petrol station | park | tourist office |
| factory | post office | railway station | town hall | bank | library | shopping centre |
| university |

MORE NEW WORDS

....

....

....

....

1. ....

2. ....

3. ....

4. ....

5. ....

6. ....

7. ....

8. ....

9. ....

| camping | photography | cooking | pottery | jewellery making | gardening |
| wood carving | stamp collecting | origami |

MORE NEW WORDS

....

....

....

....

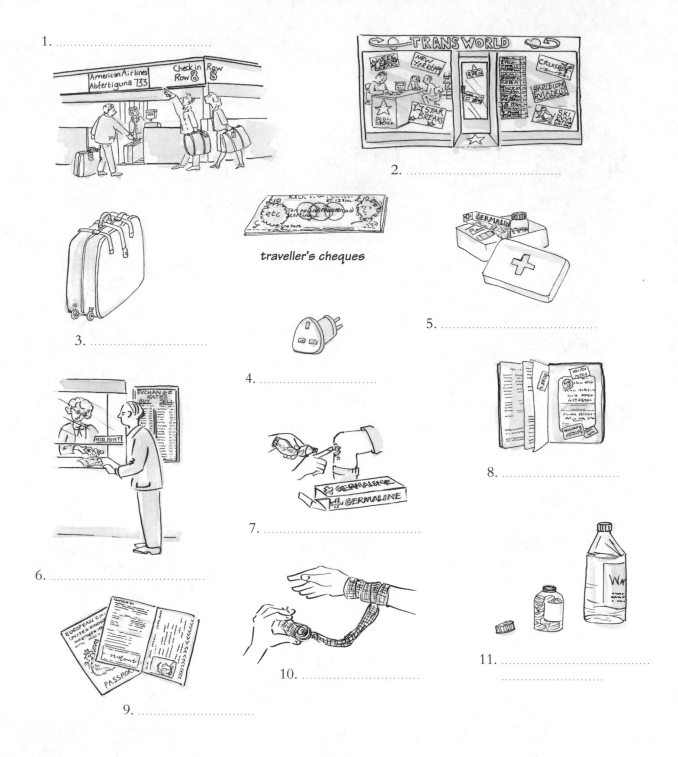

1. ....

2. ....

traveller's cheques

3. ....

4. ....

5. ....

6. ....

7. ....

8. ....

9. ....

10. ....

11. ....
....

passport	foreign currency	suitcase	first aid kit	visa	water purification tablets
bandage	check-in counter	antiseptic cream	travel agency	travel plug	

MORE NEW WORDS

....

....

....

....

I'd like …

1. ....

2. ....

3. ....

4. ....

5. ....

6. ....

7. ....

I'd like to be …

8. ....

9. ....

10. ....

11. ....

beautiful	to think	tall	to exercise	to travel	to read	time for myself	thin
a holiday	rich	to relax					

MORE NEW WORDS

....

....

....

....

1. ....

2. ....

3. ....

4. ....

5. ....

6. ....

7. ....

8. ....

9. ....

10. ....

jeweller's	chemist's	health food shop	antique shop	florist's	hairdresser's
post office	dry cleaner's	video rental shop	newsagent's		

MORE NEW WORDS

....

....

....

....

VISUAL DICTIONARY

1. ....

2. ....

3. ....

4. ....

5. ....

6. ....

7. ....

| credit card | counter | cashier | notes | bank statement | cheque | coins |

MORE NEW WORDS

....
....
....
....

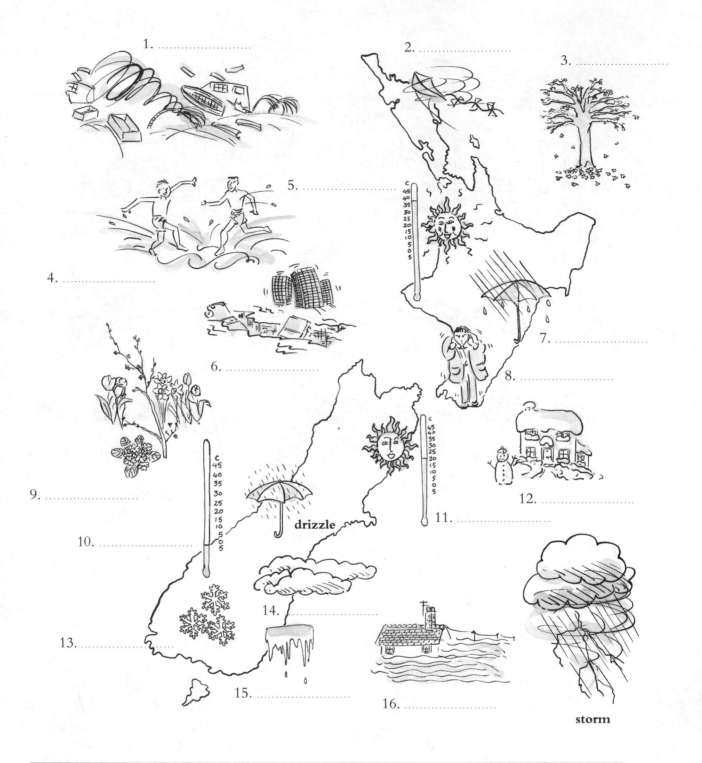

1. ....

2. ....

3. ....

4. ....

5. ....

6. ....

7. ....

8. ....

9. ....

10. ....

drizzle

11. ....

12. ....

13. ....

14. ....

15. ....

16. ....

storm

spring	summer	autumn	winter	ice	snow	rain	clouds	wind
warm	hot	cold	freezing	earthquake	flood	hurricane		

MORE NEW WORDS

....

....

....

....

1. ....

2. ....

3. ....

4. ....

5. ....

6. ....

7. ....

8. ....

9. ....
   ....

10. ....

11. ....

12. ....

wedding anniversary	candle	card	party	dance	bride	groom	gift
wedding invitation	Independence Day		Christmas		birthday cake		

MORE NEW WORDS

....

....

....

....

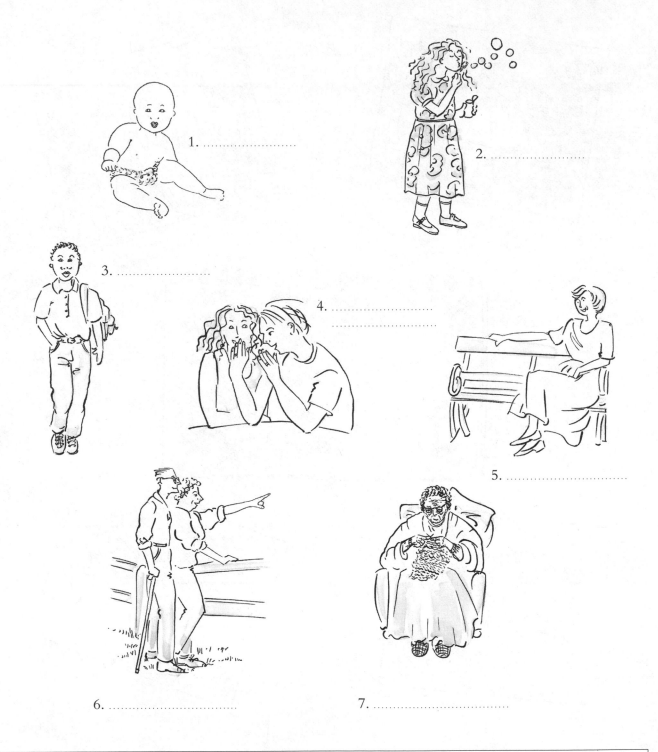

1. ....

2. ....

3. ....

4. ....
....

5. ....

6. ....

7. ....

| a child | a very old woman | a teenager | a young married couple | a middle-aged woman |
| a baby | an elderly couple | | | |

MORE NEW WORDS

....

....

....

....

TAPESCRIPTS

STARTER UNIT

Exercise 3

A
1. It's seven o'clock.
2. It's a quarter past seven.
3. It's half past three.
4. It's a quarter to four.
5. It's ten past ten.
6. It's twenty to eleven.

B
1. It's noon.   2. It's midnight.

C
1. It's twenty past nine in the morning.
2. It's half past ten in the evening.
3. It's five to two in the afternoon.
4. It's a quarter to ten in the evening.

Exercise 4

B
1. A: What time's the flight from Bangkok?
   B: Twenty-five past one.
   A: Sorry, what time?
   B: One twenty-five.
   A: Thanks a lot.
2. C: What time's the flight from Sydney, please?
   D: The flight from Sydney's at fourteen fifteen.
   C: Fourteen fifteen?
   D: Yes, that's right.
   C: Thank you.
3. E: What time's the flight from Delhi?
   F: It's at eleven thirty.
   E: Sorry, did you say eleven thirty?
   F: Yes, half-past eleven.
4. G: Excuse me, what time's the flight from Cairo, please?
   H: It arrives at Terminal Four at six fifteen.
   G: Is that six fifteen in the morning?
   H: Yes, that's right.

Exercise 5

B
Saturday the first of January; Sunday the second; Monday the third; Tuesday the fourth; Wednesday the fifth; Thursday the sixth; Friday the seventh; Saturday the eighth; Sunday the ninth; Monday the tenth
The months of the year: January, February, March, April, May, June, July, August, September, October, November, December

Exercise 8

1. A: Where's the phone?
   B: It's on the table.
   A: Where?
   B: On the table by the window.
2. C: Where's the bin?
   D: It's on the floor, under the table.
3. E: Where's the computer?
   F: It's on the desk.
   E: On the desk?
   F: On the desk, in the classroom – beside the door.
4. G: Where are the books?
   H: On the chair.
   G: Where?
   H: On the chair, next to the desk.
5. K: Where are the keys?
   L: They're in the bedroom.
   K: Where in the bedroom?
   L: On the shelf over the bed.
6. M: Where are my glasses?
   N: Um … I don't know. Oh, there they are, on the table, next to the lamp.
7. P: Where's the window?
   S: It's right there, opposite the door!

UNIT 1 FINDING OUT

Exercise 6

A
1. 13   2. 40   3. 50   4. 16

B
1. A: What does *breakfast* mean?
   B: It's a meal – in the morning.
2. A: How do you spell it?
   B: B R E A K F A S T.
3. A: Where do you come from?
   B: Japan.
   A: Whereabouts?
   B: Could you repeat that, please?
   A: Oh, whereabouts? Whereabouts in Japan do you come from?
   B: Oh, from Kyoto.
4. A: How do you say *sağol* in English?
   B: Oh, you just say *thanks*.
5. A: What time is it, please?
   B: It's half past five.
   A: I'm sorry, could you repeat that, please?
   B: Oh, it's half past five.
6. A: What page are we on, please?
   B: What exercise is it, please?
   C: It's exercise 2E on page 17.

C
1. The key for room 405, please.
2. Could I have the key for room 518, please?
3. Room 316, please.
4. The key for 613, please.

Exercise 7

A
A: What's the code for Thailand, please?
OPERATOR: Thailand … the code is 66.
B: What's the code for America?
OPERATOR: The USA? It's 1.
C: What's the code for Australia, please?
OPERATOR: It's 61.
D: The code for Finland, please.
OPERATOR: Finland … the code for Finland is 358.
E: What's the code for Dominica?
OPERATOR: Dominica?
E: Yes, the code for Dominica, please.
OPERATOR: It's 1809.

B

1. MAN: Directory enquiries, what town, please?
   WOMAN: Oxford.
   MAN: What name, please?
   WOMAN: Darby.
   MAN: Er, can you spell that?
   WOMAN: D A R B Y.
   MAN: Uhum. What's the address?
   WOMAN: 26 Rutland Avenue.
   MAN: The number is 487 8761.
2. MAN: Directory enquiries, what town, please?
   WOMAN: Minneapolis.
   MAN: And the name?
   WOMAN: Wrightson.
   MAN: Can you spell that?
   WOMAN: W R I G H T S O N.
   MAN: What's the address?
   WOMAN: 42 Main Street.
   MAN: The number is 695 7309.
3. WOMAN: Directory enquiries, what town, please?
   MAN: Edinburgh.
   WOMAN: What name, please?
   MAN: MacTavish.
   WOMAN: Would you spell that?
   MAN: Uhum. M A C T A V I S H.
   WOMAN: Uhum. MacTavish. And the address?
   MAN: It's Burns House, Dixon Road.
   WOMAN: Burns House … The number is 031 566 2389.
   MAN: Thank you.

Exercise 8

1. ARTURO: I'm from Chile, South America. What is your name?
   PAULA: My name's Paula.
   ARTURO: Paula, I am Arturo.
   PAULA: Hello, pleased to meet you.
   ARTURO: Pleased to meet you, Paula.
2. WOMAN: Hello.
   SITA: Hello.
   WOMAN: Now, what's your name?
   SITA: My name is Sita Patel.
   WOMAN: Sita Patel. And where do you come from, Sita?
   SITA: Well, I come from India.
   WOMAN: Oh, whereabouts in India?
   SITA: The northern part of India.
3. ARTURO: Good morning.
   PHILIP: Good morning.
   ARTURO: Could I ask you: what is your name?
   PHILIP: Ah, my name is Philip.
   ARTURO: Oh, Philip. Could I ask you: where are you from, Philip?
   PHILIP: I'm from the United States.
   ARTURO: Uhum … interesting. My parents come from the United States.

B

Good morning.
What's your name?
And where do you come from?

Exercise 9

This is a picture of a lady and her dog in a sitting room. In the sitting room there is a large chair, quite a lot of bookcases, with a lot of books on them. There is also a fireplace and in front of the fireplace there is a fireguard. On the floor there is a rug, and the lady is standing on the rug with the dog. She's in front of the fireplace. On the walls there are quite a lot of pictures, and on the fireplace there are quite a lot of ornaments. On the chair there is a cushion.

UNIT 2 WHAT HAVE YOU GOT?

Exercise 1

B

INTERVIEWER: Have you got a coursebook?
WOMAN: Yes.
INTERVIEWER: How many have you got?
WOMAN: Oh, just one.
INTERVIEWER: Have you got a notebook?
WOMAN: Yes, of course.
INTERVIEWER: How many have you got?
WOMAN: Just one.
INTERVIEWER: Have you got a dictionary?
WOMAN: Yes, I've got two.
INTERVIEWER: Have you got a cassette recorder?
WOMAN: No, I haven't.
INTERVIEWER: Have you got a computer?
WOMAN: Yes.
INTERVIEWER: How many have you got?
WOMAN: Oh, one, just a small one.
INTERVIEWER: Have you got a video recorder?
WOMAN: No, I haven't.
INTERVIEWER: Have you got any magazines in English?
WOMAN: Oh, no, I haven't.
INTERVIEWER: Have you got any books in English?
WOMAN: Um … yes.
INTERVIEWER: How many have you got?
WOMAN: Oh, um, I don't know … erm … four.
INTERVIEWER: Have you got any newspapers in English?
WOMAN: No, I haven't. But the library's got some.
INTERVIEWER: How many have they got?
WOMAN: Um … two.

Exercise 5

FLIGHT ATTENDANT: A drink for you?
PASSENGER: What have you got?
FLIGHT ATTENDANT: We've got coffee, tea, orange juice or mineral water.
PASSENGER: Coffee, please.
FLIGHT ATTENDANT: A drink for you?
FLIGHT ATTENDANT: We've got coffee, tea, orange juice or mineral water.
ICE CREAM VENDOR: Ice cream for you?
ICE CREAM VENDOR: I've got vanilla, chocolate and strawberry.
FLIGHT ATTENDANT: Newspaper?
FLIGHT ATTENDANT: We've got *The Times*, *The Post* and *The Express*.

Exercise 6

B

INTERVIEWER: John, have you got any family?
JOHN: Er, yes, I've got a mother, a father and a sister.
INTERVIEWER: Oh. What family have you got, Lisa?
LISA: There's just my mother and my grandmother, that's all.
INTERVIEWER: And what about you, Livia?
LIVIA: Er … let's see. I've a mother, I've got two brothers, and I've got, um, two grandparents.
INTERVIEWER: Al, have you got any children?
AL: My wife and I have got two daughters and one son.

Exercise 7

B

1. In my pocket, I've got some money. I've got a piece of string. I've got a packet of biscuits. I've got my glasses in my pocket. I've got the key to the house in my pocket. I've got my car keys in my pocket. I've got some handkerchiefs – paper ones.
2. I've got nothing in the pockets of my trousers because I've got a rather large hole in them. In the pockets of my cardigan, I've got a dirty tissue, I've got my car keys, I've got some money, and I've also got a piece of chewing gum.

UNIT 3 WHAT WOULD YOU LIKE TO EAT?

Exercise 3

C

1. In my country, America, rice and noodles and other pasta come in bags – plastic bags. Er, milk and other beverages, fruit juices, come in cartons – paper cartons. Meat … most often in supermarkets … is wrapped in cellophane.
2. In my country, Malaysia, we buy our vegetables in the open market. You take your bag along, choose your vegetables and fruit and put it in your bag. Milk comes in bottles. Spaghetti and noodles come in packets. Eggs come in boxes, and wine comes in bottles.
3. In Northern Ireland, we buy things in different types of containers. For instance, you can buy milk in a carton, but you can also buy milk in a bottle. Soup sometimes comes in tins, and it also comes in a carton. If you buy, say, apples or oranges or beans or some other sort of vegetable in the supermarket, they'll come in a packet of some kind, but if you buy them at the greengrocer's, he'll put them in a brown paper bag.

Exercise 4

B

I'd like a dozen eggs, a dozen tomatoes, a dozen oranges …
I'd like a kilo of potatoes, a kilo of peas, a kilo of beans, a kilo of apples, a kilo of carrots, a kilo of fish …
I'd like a tin of soup, a tin of tomatoes, a tin of beans …
I'd like a bottle of wine, a bottle of milk, a bottle of fruit juice …
I'd like a litre of milk, a litre of mineral water, a litre of orange juice …
I'd like a box of chocolates, a box of noodles …
I'd like half a kilo of cheese, half a kilo of rice, half a kilo of grapes, half a kilo of bananas …
I'd like half a litre of milk, half a litre of mineral water …

Exercise 5

B

1. I'd like a tin of tomatoes, please.
2. I'd like a tin of carrots, please.
3. I'd like a bottle of wine, please.
4. I'd like a carton of milk, please.
5. I'd like a packet of spaghetti, please.
6. I'd like a kilo of peas, please.
7. I'd like a kilo of bananas, please.
8. I'd like a box of chocolates, please.
9. I'd like a bag of potatoes, please.
10. I'd like a bottle of orange juice, please.

Exercise 6

B

1. CUSTOMER: How much is this pineapple?
   STALL KEEPER: It's $2.
2. CUSTOMER: How much are these bananas?
   STALL KEEPER: Um … they're $5 a kilo.
3. CUSTOMER: And those?
   STALL KEEPER: $4 a kilo, but they're not so nice.
4. CUSTOMER: How much is that bottle of mineral water?
   STALL KEEPER: The litre bottle is $3.
5. CUSTOMER: And this one?
   STALL KEEPER: $5 – it comes from France.
6. CUSTOMER: How much is this?
   STALL KEEPER: The orange juice?
   CUSTOMER: Yes.
   STALL KEEPER: Um … $2, I think. George, how much is the orange juice? The Brazilian orange juice is $2.
7. CUSTOMER: How much are those tomatoes?
   STALL KEEPER: Tomatoes are $5 a kilo this week.
8. CUSTOMER: How about those over there?
   STALL KEEPER: They're on special offer – $3 a kilo.
9. CUSTOMER: And that cheese, how much is it?
   STALL KEEPER: It's very expensive – it's from Switzerland.

Exercise 7

A

1. I like Indian food. Um … a mild curry is usually what I have, and it's usually vegetable.
2. I like Chinese food, because I'm a vegetarian and I find that their combination of vegetables is very tasty.
3. My favourite Asian food comes from India. I really like Indian restaurants because they have lots of fish dishes. And I'm not vegetarian but I don't eat meat, only fish.

UNIT 4 A SENSE OF COLOUR

Exercise 1

1. Where do you buy your shoes?
2. Where do you buy your sweaters?
3. Where do you buy your jeans?
4. Where do you buy your socks?
5. How often do you buy shoes?
6. How often do you buy hats?

Exercise 3

A

Example:
Q: Do you prefer brown or black shoes?
A: Brown.
1. Do you prefer blue or black jeans?
2. Do you prefer your coffee black or white?
3. Do you prefer black T-shirts or white ones?

B
4. Does your friend prefer blue or black jeans?
5. Does your friend prefer black or white coffee?
6. Does your friend prefer black T-shirts or white ones?

Exercise 4

blue sky   green grass   red fire   a grey cloud
an orange traffic light   a black cat   a brown dog
a pink flamingo   a gold ring   a yellow lemon

Exercise 5

B

MAN: Jackie, tell me, what colours are fashionable in Ireland this year?

JACKIE: Er, well, of course green is always fashionable.

MAN: Oh, yes.

JACKIE: The Irish love green and I think red, red this year. What about in America?

MAN: Oh, I'd say we like checks and blues, actually, this year.

JACKIE: Hmm.

MAN: Sorry, I was going to say, at work, do people prefer to wear kind of fashionable clothes or conventional clothes?

JACKIE: Um, I think probably conventional clothes at work, yes, definitely conventional clothes. What about in America?

MAN: Well, in America, they may want to wear fashionable clothes, but they're often forced to wear conventional clothes. And on holiday, er, we kind of like shorts and T-shirts, that sort of thing. How about with you?

JACKIE: I think it's the same. On holiday everyone wears their comfortable clothes, really.

MAN: But when it comes to suits, in your country are they mostly fashionable or conventional?

JACKIE: Oh, well, I think fashionable. The Irish think they are a very fashionable race.

MAN: And in America, we just wear suits in the workplace. So they're mainly conventional. Do men and women in your country prefer fashionable shoes or comfortable shoes?

JACKIE: Well, I think probably fashionable shoes, but then if you're wearing a shoe it has to be comfortable, doesn't it? But I think fashionable, yes, mainly.

MAN: Well, we're mainly too heavy for fashionable shoes, so we tend to wear comfortable shoes.

Exercise 6

1. My jackets are made in Japan. They're made of leather.
2. Your blouses are made in Brazil. They're made of polyester.
3. His ties are made in Thailand. They're made of silk.
4. Her skirts are made in Scotland. They're made of wool.
5. Our raincoats are made in Romania. They're made of nylon.
6. Their shirts are made in Sri Lanka. They're made of cotton.

Exercise 7

1. As I come from the northwest part of my country, the colours that are most noticeable in the countryside are dark green, because of the kinds of trees that grow. And it remains dark green all year round. Of course, then there is the earth colours of the, the roads, if they are dirt roads. And, er, then there is the blue of the sky. Flower colours? Many many different kinds of colours … in my country.
   The colours of the flag? Red white and blue.
2. In my country, the colour depends on the time of the year. The colour of the countryside, I mean. Before the monsoons, everything is dusty and brown and red. Even the green trees are covered in red dust. But after the monsoon, everything's lush and green and bright.
   Most of the buildings, people's houses and public buildings, are painted white. Flowers come in many colours – whole trees are covered in flowers: reds, blues, orange, purple, yellow …
   And the colours of the flag: red, green, orange and white.

UNIT 5 GOOD HABITS, NEW ROUTINES?

Exercise 1

A

1. What time do you get up in the morning? *or*
   What time do you leave the house?
2. How often do you have a cup of tea? *or*
   How often do you have a meal?
3. How often do you go on holiday? *or*
   How often do you go away?
4. Why does he go shopping in the market? *or*
   Why does he cook curry?
5. What does she do at nine? *or*
   Why does she know so much?

C

1. Does he do the cooking? *or*
   Does he spend his weekends at home?
2. Does she go out a lot? *or*
   Does she use the car?
3. Where do you buy vegetables? *or*
   Where do you go shopping?

Exercise 6

B

1. INTERVIEWER: Do you read travel books?
   ALEX: Yes, I do.
   INTERVIEWER: Why?
   ALEX: I very much like travelling to other countries, so often I read a few books to give me a few ideas about where I could go for my holidays.
2. INTERVIEWER: Do you shout at other people?
   BRIDGET: I'm afraid I do, yes.
   INTERVIEWER: Why?
   BRIDGET: Because I'm a very bad-tempered, horrible person!
3. INTERVIEWER: Joan, do you get up early on Sundays?
   JOAN: No, I don't.
   INTERVIEWER: Why not?
   JOAN: Because the rest of my week is very ordered and I have to get up early and do things at a certain time and Sunday is the only chance I have to really laze about. And I usually start my day by reading the papers in bed.
4. INTERVIEWER: Do you spend a lot of money when you're on holiday?
   ROD: Well, I'm not quite sure how much everybody else spends, but I think I probably do spend quite a lot.
   INTERVIEWER: Why is that?
   ROD: Well, it's partly because my main holiday is usually skiing and skiing is a very expensive occupation.
5. INTERVIEWER: Nick, do you tidy your house or your flat every day?
   NICK: No, I don't.
   INTERVIEWER: Why not?
   NICK: Um … because I'm too lazy, I think.
6. INTERVIEWER: Do you eat fast food?
   NED: No, I don't.
   INTERVIEWER: Why is that?
   NED: Um, I don't think it's that good for you.

UNIT 6 THE WAY YOU LOOK

Exercise 4

A

legs chest hand neck bag man men jacket back

B

1. A: I've got some sunglasses for your eyes.
   B: They're too dark!
2. A: I've got some socks for your feet.
   B: They're not large enough!
3. A: I've got a scarf for your neck.
   B: It's too long!
4. A: I've got a hat for your head.
   B: It's not big enough!
5. A: I've got some gloves for your hands.
   B: They're too small!
6. A: I've got some shoes for your feet.
   B: They're pink!

Exercise 5

B

1. I think eyes are really important. Lively eyes … you know, they say a lot about your personality, eyes. When I meet people, I look at their eyes first. Oh, and I think nice, clean hair is important too. Untidy hair doesn't make a very good impression, especially at work.

2. For me, a big smile is what's important. That's what makes a nice appearance. A happy face makes other people feel happy too. Well, and … of course eyes are important too. You smile with your eyes as well as your mouth, I think. But, I don't think hair is very important at all. Some nice people don't even have very much hair, after all …

Exercise 7

A

JUANITA: Well, I think a job as a hotel receptionist is right for me because, um, well, I've got the right qualifications. Um, I speak English and Spanish, and, um, I think I'm quite intelligent, and I work hard. Oh, and people say that I'm lively and happy. I think that's important for a receptionist, because, um, well, you work with people.

UNIT 7 WHAT CAN WE DO?

Exercise 7

A

1. Can you read in a car?
2. Can you type?
3. Can you cook a good meal?
4. Can you write a poem?
5. Can you stand on your head?
6. Can you drive a car?

B

1. Can you read in a car?
   No, I can't. I get sick.
2. Can you type?
   Yes, I can. I can type very quickly, with two fingers.
3. Can you cook a good meal?
   Yes, I can. I can do it in twenty minutes.
4. Can you write a poem?
   No, I can't. I can't think of rhymes.
5. Can you stand on your head?
   Yes, of course I can. I can stand on my head for five minutes.
6. Can you drive a car?
   Well, of course I can. I can even fly a plane.

Exercise 8

MOTHER: Hello, son. Good day at school?
SON: Fine, Mum. Er, can you come here for a second?
MOTHER: Yeah. What's the problem?
SON: Isn't life wonderful? I just want to say that, in spite of everything, I love you.
MOTHER: Are you feeling all right, son?
SON: Very funny, Mum.
MOTHER: OK. Let me guess. How much do you want?
SON: Can you sign my report card? Please?
MOTHER: How come you have only three As on your report card?
SON: No problem, Mum. I can pass this year easily.
MOTHER: Pass? Passing isn't enough! In Korea, students of your age study all day because they want to have a good life!
SON: But this isn't Korea, Mum. Do you want me to study all day?
MOTHER: I didn't say that. I want you to study and have good marks. I want you to have a good life in the future.
SON: A pass is a pass. What's the difference? This is the 90s. The world's changed. My friends have got bad marks too.
MOTHER: I don't care about that. I really want to give you a good life. Can't you at least study a bit more?

UNIT 8 LOVE IT OR HATE IT!

Exercise 3

B

1. Do you like cats?
2. Do you like dogs?
3. Do you like horses?
4. How about goats?
5. Do you like mosquitoes?
6. How about snakes?
7. Do you like spiders?
8. Do you like cockroaches?
9. What about flies?
10. What animals do you like, then?

Exercise 4

B

1. The frog's on the log.
2. The dog's in the fog.
3. The goat's in the boat.
4. The hippo's at the disco.
5. The mosquito's on my toe.
6. Show me the way to go home.

Exercise 6

A

1. On the weekends most of all I like to sleep in, I must admit, because I work so hard during the week that, er, Saturday mornings are the one time I get to sleep in. And on Sunday I go roller skating, generally.
2. At the weekend, um, I usually take the children swimming in the morning and then, um, we watch some television and er … sometimes go to the market in the afternoon.
3. On Saturdays I usually wake up quite early. Then I usually go and get the papers and have breakfast.
4. On Saturday I normally do my shopping, which is something that I don't really like doing. And then in the afternoon I take my child to the park. On Sunday I like to have a nice long breakfast and I buy the newspaper.

B

1. Well, what I really hate is washing up. And, er, I always try to find somebody else to do it. And another thing I can't stand is sitting on a bus behind a long row of traffic …
2. Mm, I hate driving in traffic when you're sitting in a long queue behind a lot of silly drivers who are doing completely the wrong things. Erm, I also hate doing the washing. I mean, I know it's only putting things in the washing machine but that really gets to me, I don't like that.
3. I don't mind any of that, really. But what I can't stand is spiders. I've never been able to get on with them. And it's the way they move. It frightens me and I, I just hate them.
4. I don't mind spiders. I hate cockroaches, though. They're, they're disgusting. I hate them.

Exercise 8

INTERVIEWER: Right, can you tell us, do you like living here?
GERTRUDE: Yes, otherwise I wouldn't be here because, um, I made a choice coming here, so … yes, I like it very much.
INTERVIEWER: Um, what is it you like about living in a different culture?
GERTRUDE: Um, well, I think you see things more clearly, you notice more things, if you're an outsider.
INTERVIEWER: Right. I think I know the answer, but are you a cheerful kind of person?
GERTRUDE: Well, um, yes, I think so.
INTERVIEWER: Er, and … travel? Do you love travel?
GERTRUDE: Yes, I love travelling.
INTERVIEWER: Right. And foods? Er, do you love trying new foods?
GERTRUDE: Yes, yes … which is very easy to do in London … anyway.
INTERVIEWER: And how do you find this out? Do you read a lot about this country?
GERTRUDE: No, I don't really read about England. I read, erm, English literature … but not about England.
INTERVIEWER: Great. Thank you very much.
GERTRUDE: Thank you.
INTERVIEWER: Jean-Pierre, do you like living here?
JEAN-PIERRE: Yes, I do.
INTERVIEWER: Why is that?
JEAN-PIERRE: I think it's because of the incredible variety one, one gets in, er, London, basically.
INTERVIEWER: What do you like about living in a different culture?
JEAN-PIERRE: I think I basically like the, the difference at all levels.
INTERVIEWER: Are you a cheerful kind of person?
JEAN-PIERRE: I think I am, yes.
INTERVIEWER: Yes. And do you love travel?
JEAN-PIERRE: I do love travel, yes.
INTERVIEWER: So, on your travels, do you like trying new foods?
JEAN-PIERRE: I certainly do.
INTERVIEWER: Do you read a lot about this country?
JEAN-PIERRE: No, I don't. I think I experience it more than I read about it.

UNIT 9 THOSE WERE THE DAYS

Exercise 5

1. Did you use the phone yesterday?
2. Did your parents hate your clothes when you were a teenager?
3. Did you like your years at secondary school?
4. Did your friends like playing sports at school?
5. Did you hate going to bed early as a child?
6. Did you listen to the question before this one?

Exercise 6

D

1. There are no sharks in the sea near England or Germany.
2. A shark can't swim fast enough to reach Sydney in ten days.
3. In a shark's stomach, a newspaper falls to pieces.
4. A fisherman is not strong enough to pull in a big shark by hand.

Exercise 7

C

1. C: It was October the 3rd
   D: No, no, it wasn't, it was the 4th.
   C: No, you're wrong, it was the 3rd.
   D: Well, if you remember, the 3rd was the Saturday, cos it was Jeannie's birthday.
   C: No, that was the Friday, it was the 3rd.
   D: No, no, the Sunday was the 4th. That's the day we're talking about, isn't it?
   C: No, we're talking about the Friday.
2. E: She was a great boss.
   F: Are you crazy? She was a dragon … always watching the clock.
   E: She was lovely.
   F: She was mean to me.
   E: That's because you were always late.
3. G: They were yellow.
   H: No, they weren't, they were orange!
   G: You call that orange? They were yellow!
   H: Are you blind? They were orange, I tell you!
   G: OK, we'll have to agree to disagree.
   H: Pardon?

UNIT 10 ONCE UPON A TIME

Exercise 3

What did I do last week? Erm … oh, well, on Saturday I met a friend and we went to the theatre together, in the afternoon. We saw this, oh, wonderful musical … great music … we really enjoyed it. So, at the end we got up and left, and of course, I forgot all about my umbrella, under the seat. So, off we went, and we thought, um, oh, well, let's have a bite to eat. So we found this little café and we sat outside at these tables and had a coffee, and, um, er, a sandwich. And suddenly it began to rain, you know, it just poured – and I thought Aaaah, my umbrella! So, I ran all the way back to the theatre, and sure enough, they had it there; I was lucky, but I was already pretty wet … soaking wet, in fact.

Exercise 4

The fisherman comes home
And did you catch a fish, son?
I caught a lot.
And did you buy a lemon?
Oh, I forgot.
And did you clean the fish, then?
It was too hot.
Well, did you have a nice day?
Oh, I just sat.
And did you bring the fish home?
Er … I fed the cat.
And what about our meal then?
Can't you do that?
I'll show you what I *can* do!
'My head!' he said.

Exercise 5

1. 'The first sunrise', a legend from Australia
   Once, long ago, the sky was very close to the earth, and people walked on their hands and knees. They could not stand up. The magpies were intelligent birds. They thought they could raise the sky. They got sticks and pushed. They raised the sky a little bit, and then they got big stones and rested the sky on them. People stood up. The birds raised the sky again. Suddenly it split open, and people saw the first beautiful sunrise. The magpies started singing. After that, the birds always sang at sunrise.

2. 'How the birds made the world', from the Pacific Coast of Canada
   Once upon a time the world was shut up inside a big shell, like an oyster. The birds flew over the big shell. They saw that the world was closed, they heard the people inside shouting. They got large stones and dropped them on the shell. The shell opened up a little bit. The birds caught the edge of the shell with their beaks and pulled. The shell split open and people ran out into the sunlight. The birds flew away and left the people in their new world.

Exercise 6

C

1. When did the study of fossils begin?
2. Why are there no dinosaurs?
3. Why did all the dinosaurs die?
4. Who invented the word *dinosaur*?
5. When did Richard Owen invent the word *dinosaur*?
6. Could dinosaurs run?
7. What did some dinosaurs have to protect them?
8. What did dinosaurs eat?

Exercise 7

POLICEWOMAN: Can you tell us what happened, sir?
MAN: Well, I went down to the market on Monday the 9th of October. It was around ten in the morning, I guess. I was on the corner of Market Street and Main Street, when suddenly this car came round the corner very fast and crashed straight into a fruit stand. There was this great crashing noise, and the stand shattered into pieces, and, um, this poor lady was there by the stand, and the car hit her, I guess, and knocked her to the ground. I, I didn't really see that; I ran to get out of the way. There was fruit everywhere, apples and bananas and pineapples – in the street, over the car, just everywhere.

UNIT 11 WHAT'S GOING ON?

Exercise 5

A

1. PAUL: Our reporter, Julia Strecki, is in the city, and sends us this report.
   JULIA: Hello, Paul … I'm standing here in the central square and I'm afraid things are looking very bad. There's thick smoke everywhere, the lava is beginning to pour down the side of Mount Etna. People are packing up everything they can and leaving the city. The roads are full of people trying to get away …
2. ANNOUNCER: We go now to Derya Patlin in Dallas. She's waiting to describe the scene as the President begins his visit to the city.
   DERYA: The whole city is waiting for the President's car to appear. There are many people waiting by the side of the road, some waving flags. And here he is … I can just see the car; it's turning into the main road … The President is sitting in the back seat beside the First Lady. They're both smiling and waving to the crowds. She's wearing a (shots) … there's … there's … it's a shot … I can't see … I think … yes, the President's been hit; he's slumping forwards …
3. REPORTER: I'm down here on the beach. The big white monster is now quite close on the water, and I can see that it's got two parts – a dark part near the bottom and the very big white thing at the top. And now a small, er, it looks a bit like a boat – yes, it's a kind of boat, and it's leaving the monster and coming over the water to us. Many people are waiting on the beach. They're obviously frightened. Some are waving their hands … some are shouting … And now we can see that the boat has got some people in it … I, I think they're people … but very strange. They're wearing very strange-coloured clothes – like coloured birds – and their skin is very white … And now, they're getting out of the boat … and coming onto the beach. Our people are moving back in fear …

UNIT 12 MAKING PLANS

Exercise 4

A

1. What are you doing this weekend, Alex?
   I'm making a cake, and I'm going to the lake.
2. What are you doing this weekend, Pat?
   I'm reading a book, and I'm learning to cook.
3. What are you doing this weekend, Olivia?
   I'm buying a hat, and I'm getting a cat.
4. What are you doing this weekend, Tony?
   I'm going to the beach, and I'm buying a peach.
5. What are you doing this weekend, you two?
   I'm playing a game, and she's doing the same.

Exercise 5

1. Peter Middleton is a Chief Executive for Thomas Cook. He's going to Indonesia for ten days. He lived there for two years twenty years ago. It's partly a business tour of the Far East – his family's going to join him there. He's not going to lie on the beach – he doesn't like sunbathing.
2. Mike Smith is a doctor. His wife and he are going to Corsica. They're going for the fresh air, and the sailing. They're not going to lie on the beach and it's certainly not good for people, especially at their age.
3. Anne Winterton is a Member of Parliament, an MP. She's going to Portugal for two or three weeks in September. She and her family go there every year. It's informal and they can get away from the pressures of work.
4. Eamonn Fahey delivers eggs, and also works in a theatre. He's going to Malta for two weeks with his girlfriend because he's got an apartment there. They're going to lie on the beach and go to discos and relax. They go there because there aren't many places left where the English are really liked.
5. Cliff Michelmore is a travel broadcaster. He's not going to go anywhere. He comes from the Isle of Wight. He lives there and loves it. He and his family spend their time there and take their holidays there too.
6. Caroline Dawney, is a literary agent, and this year, as usual, she's going bicycling with her son in Somerset. She goes on holiday to get her son, who's 11, away from his computer. They're going to stay at lovely bed and breakfast places and they're going to enjoy meeting new dogs.

UNIT 13 BETTER AND BETTER

Exercise 5

In picture B, the table is a bit bigger. The parasol above it is a lot smaller than in A. In picture A, the jug on the table is smaller than the cup, but in picture B, the jug is much bigger than the cup. The book next to the cup is a bit bigger in picture B. The flowers in picture A are much smaller.

Exercise 6

1. Shall I compare you to a forest? You are darker and more mysterious.
2. Shall I compare you to a mango? You're softer and more expensive.
3. Shall I compare you to a computer? You are more calculating and more boring.

UNIT 14 A SPIRIT OF ADVENTURE

Exercise 2

1. MAN: It's stopped raining.
   WOMAN: Yes, I think you're right.
2. WOMAN: The taxi's arrived!
   MAN: OK, I'm coming!
3. MAN: I've lost my car keys.
   WOMAN: Are you sure? Go through your pockets again.
4. WOMAN: They've taken my camera!
   MAN: Yes, and my computer … it was new!

Exercise 3

1. Have you ever slept all night on a beach?
   No, never.
2. Have you ever visited a camel farm?
   A camel farm? No, I haven't.
3. Have you ever played basketball?
   Yes, lots of times.
4. Have you ever spent some time in hospital?
   Yes, I have, about ten years ago.
5. Have you ever stayed in an expensive hotel?
   Yes, I have, lots of times.
6. Have you ever been to Nepal?
   I haven't, no.
7. Have you ever lost all your money?
   I have, yes, once.

Exercise 6

Have you done your homework?
I'm sorry but I haven't had time.

Have you started the washing up?
Have you done the shopping?
Has she cleaned the car?
Have you had something to eat?
Have they brought the books back?

Have you done your homework?
I'm sorry but I haven't had time.
Have you started the washing up?
I'm sorry but I haven't had time.
Have you done the shopping?
I'm sorry but I haven't had time.
Has she cleaned the car?
I'm sorry but she hasn't had time.
Have you had something to eat?
I'm sorry but I haven't had time.
Have they brought the books back?
I'm sorry but they haven't had time.

Exercise 7

1. DOCTOR: Come in and take a seat, Mr Green … How are you today?
   MR GREEN: Not too bad, thanks, doctor, but I've got a bit of a pain in my back.
   DOCTOR: Mmm. OK. Whereabouts is the pain? Can you show me?
2. PATIENT: It's probably nothing, I'm sorry to bother you.
   DOCTOR: Don't worry, just try to tell me what the problem is. Take your time.
   PATIENT: Well, it's my throat. It's been really sore for weeks now. I've taken throat sweets, but it keeps coming back. Do you think it's serious?
3. DOCTOR: How have you been lately?
   PATIENT: Really tired. There's so much happening at work, and what with my husband and the children, and my mother's illness, I feel really stressed and it's all getting too much for me. I just don't know what to do, I really don't.
   DOCTOR: Mmm. Are you sleeping all right?

Exercise 8

MAN: Have you ever been to a soccer match?
WOMAN: No, I don't like soccer, it's boring.
MAN: Oh. Well, what about cricket? Have you ever watched that?
WOMAN: Yes, I have actually. I once had a boyfriend who was mad on cricket and he once took me to see a match between England and Australia … somewhere in Manchester, I think.
MAN: Did you enjoy it?
WOMAN: Yes, I did actually … I didn't watch much cricket, but the weather was wonderful and we had some really nice sandwiches. What about you? Have you ever watched an interesting sport?
MAN: Erm, yes, I have … I once went to the races.
WOMAN: Was it good?
MAN: Well, I love animals, so it was nice to see all the beautiful race horses, but one horse got killed in a race so I came home very sad, and I've never been again.
WOMAN: Any others? What about skiing? Have you ever watched that?
MAN: I've seen ski races on TV a few times. They're really exciting aren't they? Because there's only a few seconds' difference in time between so many skiers, so you're never sure who is going to win.
WOMAN: Mmm. I like to watch skiing too … it's much cheaper than doing it too.
MAN: That's true.
WOMAN: Have you ever watched Japanese sumo wrestling on TV?
MAN: Yes, it's great, isn't it?
WOMAN: Do you think so? I don't like it … I don't really understand it … it's so quick and those men they're so …
MAN: Fat?
WOMAN: … big!

UNIT 15 DOES BEING TIDY SAVE TIME?

Exercise 1

Example:
Do you dislike working in an untidy place?
Oh, yes. I hate working in an untidy place. I always tidy my desk before starting work.

1. Do you keep making lists?
   Yes, I do. I'm always making lists for everything – shopping, things to do at work. It stops me from forgetting things.
2. Do you enjoy having a deadline?
   Oh, absolutely. I not only enjoy having a deadline, I can't seem to start anything without one.
3. Do you like writing things down in a diary?
   Yes, I do. Writing things down in a diary is important in my job, but I also have a diary to plan my life at home. I write everything down, absolutely everything.
4. Do you keep forgetting appointments?
   No. I never forget appointments. Never.
5. Do you prefer paying your bills immediately?
   Of course. As soon as I receive the bill, I open it, get out my cheque book and pay. Leaving bills is a dangerous thing, I think.
6. Do you like knowing exactly how much money you've got?
   I do, yes. Knowing exactly how much money I've got is important to me, so I look at all my bank statements very carefully.

Here is your profile for the questionnaire.
If you've got six *yes* answers: You are very well organised. You like being tidy and systematic in everything you do.
If you've got between three and six *yes* answers: You are quite well organised. Sometimes you have problems when you forget things, but most of the time you manage.
If you've got under 3 *yes* answers: I'm afraid you're not very well organised. But perhaps you prefer having an interesting time, and don't like being tidy and organised. You are probably creative or artistic.

Exercise 3

1. I read for a while … no, er, the very last thing I do is switch off the light.
2. Usually I just say my name.
3. I have a good strong cup of coffee to wake up with, then I'm ready to face all the things on my desk.
4. I look through all the letters and then, er, I water all the plants in the kitchen.

1. What's the last thing you do before going to sleep?
   I read for a while … no, er, the very last thing I do is switch off the light.
2. What's the first thing you say after picking up the phone?
   Usually I just say my name.
3. What's the first thing you do before starting work in the morning?
   I have a good strong cup of coffee to wake up with, then I'm ready to face all the things on my desk.
4. What's the first thing you do after getting home from a long holiday?
   I look through all the letters and then, er, I water all the plants in the kitchen.

Exercise 6

JULIA: Well, old business cards are handy for writing notes on …
MIKE: Yes, yes, that's a good idea.
JULIA: They're also good for putting a drink on …
BOB: Mm, I do that sometimes.
SARA: Or for planning a short talk. You can write notes for each part of the talk on a different card.
JULIA: Mmm, great idea
SARA: What about old mugs?
MIKE: Well, old mugs are handy for storing things like pens and pencils or paper clips; that's about all, isn't it?
SARA: Well, they're good for keeping things like rubber bands, for instance, because you can put the rubber band around the mug.
BOB: Mm, I suppose so.
JULIA: Old telephone books are useful for putting computers on; they're also good for standing on to reach things.
ALL: Mmm.
SARA: They're handy for keeping the door open too on a windy day.
MIKE: Mmm, you're right.

UNIT 16 OUR NEIGHBOURHOOD

Exercise 6

A
The university   The department store

1. the library   2. the petrol station   3. the tourist office
4. the railway station   5. the shopping centre

B
1. Go along the street past the medical centre on the left. What's the next building?
2. Go towards the end of the street. What's opposite the university?
3. Go along the street. What's the first building on the right?
4. What's the building before the car park?
5. What's opposite the post office?

1. Go along the street past the medical centre on the left. What's the next building?
   The department store.
2. Go towards the end of the street. What's opposite the university?
   The post office.
3. Go along the street. What's the first building on the right?
   The tourist office.
4. What's the building before the car park?
   The shopping centre.
5. What's opposite the post office?
   The university.

Exercise 7

MIKE: Jackie, have you read the paper yet today?
JACKIE: No, I haven't had time.
MIKE: What about you, Stephen?
STEPHEN: Just the headlines.
MIKE: And Dave?
DAVE: Yes, I've read a bit of it.
MIKE: Well then, Stephen, have you been to the bank yet today, or this week?
STEPHEN: Well, in fact on Wednesday I went.
MIKE: Ah. Jackie, have you been to the bank this week?
JACKIE: Yes, I went today.
MIKE: What about you, Dave.
DAVE: No, not this week.
MIKE: Then, Dave, have you done the shopping yet this week?
DAVE: Ah, no, I haven't.
MIKE: No? Jackie?
JACKIE: No, I haven't either.
MIKE: Stephen, have you, er, done the shopping yet this week?
STEPHEN: Just the odd thing. Yeah.
MIKE: Stephen, have you had a holiday yet this year?
STEPHEN: We went at Easter.
MIKE: Oh. Jackie?
JACKIE: No, I'm going next week.
MIKE: What about you, Dave?
DAVE: Yes, luckily, two.
MIKE: Mm. Er, Jackie, have you paid an electricity bill yet this year?
JACKIE: Yes, I've paid three electricity bills this year.
MIKE: Stephen, have you paid an electricity bill yet this year?
STEPHEN: I've just had one, it was enormous!
MIKE: Ah. What about you, Dave?
DAVE: Er, not yet paid, I'm afraid.

UNIT 17 IT'S WORTH DOING WELL

Exercise 5

ALAN: How would you describe good language learners, Jane?
JANE: That's a big question!
ALAN: Mm, it is, isn't it?
JANE: Well, erm, I think good learners are very active, they like using the new language and use it confidently … they don't worry about mistakes because they know they learn from mistakes.
ALAN: Mm, that's very true.
JANE: They busily explore the language … all the time trying to understand more about it.
ALAN: Yes, and another thing is the cultural side. In my experience, good learners always seem to be interested in people. Of course, they want to understand the language, but they are also interested in understanding the people who use it in their countries and, er, why they say things, why they talk to each other in certain ways, so it's not just what they say.
JANE: Mm, that's very true. They take their learning seriously in that way, don't they? And they're not just learning the language to speak it. I think good learners are also patient … they learn patiently, because they know it takes time. They can be quick learners, but they know that to know a language, well, takes many months, years.
ALAN: All your life, in fact, we're still learning about English, well, I am.
JANE: Oh, me too! Yes, that's true, your own language is changing all the time, so you never stop learning about it.

UNIT 18 ON YOUR TRAVELS

Exercise 4

MAN: Do you have a half price ticket to Africa?
WOMAN: Half price?
MAN: Yes, on TV you advertised half price travel to Africa.
WOMAN: Half price travel?
MAN: Yes, it was an offer for everyone over 45.
WOMAN: Over 45?
MAN: Yes, I'm 55 and so are my five friends.
WOMAN: You've got five friends?
MAN: Yes, so can we have five half price special travel offer tickets for Africa, please?
WOMAN: Sorry, the offer finished five days ago.
MAN: That's not very fair, we'll have to travel full fare now.
WOMAN: That's life, I'm afraid!

Exercise 5

1. WOMAN: I went to the embassy.
   MAN: Oh, why?
   WOMAN: To find out about the situation in Egypt and the Middle East.
2. MAN: You should go to South America.
   WOMAN: Mm, I know. It sounds interesting. Have you ever been to the United States?
   MAN: Only for a few hours when I stopped in Los Angeles on the way to Sao Paulo.
3. Passengers should go to the check-in counter and then go immediately to gate 7 where Flight 798 to Tokyo is now boarding.
4. WOMAN: I have to go to the station now.
   MAN: Oh, why?
   WOMAN: I'm meeting a client.
   MAN: At the station?
   WOMAN: Yes, I have to go to platform 8 and meet the 10 o'clock train from Vienna.
5. MO: Nine nine two, oh six oh four, hello?
   SUE: Oh, Mo, did I get you up? Were you in bed already?
   MO: Yeah … I'm really tired.
   SUE: Had a hard day?
   MO: Well, just a long day. I had to get up early to go to work. Phone calls all morning. I went to the travel agency at lunchtime and got my tickets. After work I went to school – you know I'm learning Spanish – and after that I had to go to the hotel to meet this client. Then I got home and I just went to bed.
6. MAN 1: Where's the duty-free shop?
   MAN 2: To go to the duty-free shop, you just go down to the exit, do you see, over there, and turn right. There's a sign.

Exercise 6

BILL: Excuse me, could you fill in this form for me, please, I can't write with this bandaged hand?
KARIN: Sure.
BILL: My name's Bill, by the way.
KARIN: I'm Karin, glad to meet you. OK. Can you tell me your family name?
BILL: It's Spencer. S P E N C E R.
KARIN: OK, and your given name is Bill?
BILL: No, you'd better put William. W I LL I A M.
KARIN: And your country of citizenship?
BILL: I'm British.
KARIN: Mm. OK. And your passport number?
BILL: Wait a minute. It's 532675E.
KARIN: Where and when were you born?
BILL: In Singapore on the 17th August, 1973.
KARIN: OK, you're male so I'll tick that box. Are you married?

BILL: No, I'm still single.

KARIN: OK, erm, are you a visitor or a resident?

BILL: I'm a resident, I live in Australia now.

KARIN: Uh huh, and are you leaving permanently?

BILL: No, I'm only going to visit my parents.

KARIN: How long will you be away?

BILL: One month. That's the longest time I can get off from my job.

KARIN: It asks what is the main reason for going abroad. Shall I put 'visiting relatives'?

BILL: Yes, that's fine.

KARIN: Where are you going to spend most of that month?

BILL: In Portugal actually, my parents don't live in England any more … they moved to Portugal when they retired.

KARIN: Sounds nice. Where in Australia do you live?

BILL: Sydney.

KARIN: And your occupation?

BILL: I'm a chef in a hotel.

KARIN: OK. I can do the rest because I think we're on the same flight BA 009 from Sydney to London.

BILL: Yeah, that's right.

KARIN: And it's July 12th today. Do you think you can sign this?

BILL: I think so. Can you put the pen in my hand … thanks.

KARIN: What happened to your hand?

UNIT 19 A LOOK AT LIFE!

Exercise 5

INTERVIEWER: Ian would you like to be more intelligent?

IAN: No, I don't think I would really, no.

INTERVIEWER: Why not?

IAN: Well, I think I'm very intelligent as it is, and I get very stressed and very worn out and I think if I was any more intelligent than I actually am, I'd go mad.

INTERVIEWER: I see.

INTERVIEWER: Would you like to be more intelligent?

LYN: Well, I think sometimes I would, because, erm, I went to college but I always felt like I was, er, not one of the brightest ones in the college and I always felt a little bit inadequate because of that …

INTERVIEWER: Ian, would you like to be a woman?

IAN: Well, yes, I would actually, yes, mm.

INTERVIEWER: Why?

IAN: Well, I've got five children, and they're sort of all under ten, yet I don't feel very close to them; my wife does and I think if, if I were a woman, I think the bond would be greater. Yes, I would, would like to be a woman.

INTERVIEWER: Lyn, would you like to be a man?

LYN: Well, I spent my young life wanting to be a man because it seemed to me that men's activities were always more fun than women's, but as I got older, I'm actually quite proud to be a woman, and when I look at men's activities now, they, they don't seem that rich really; so I think I'm happy to stay as I am.

UNIT 20 I'M SO SORRY!

Exercise 1

1. CUSTOMER: Excuse me, waiter, I'm afraid this coffee's cold.

   WAITER: Oh, I'm very sorry, madam. You can have another cup, of course.

2. CUSTOMER: I bought these shoes last week. If you look, you can see the heel's already worn down. Can you do anything?

   SHOP ASSISTANT: I'm sorry about that, madam. Have you got your receipt, please?

3. CUSTOMER: Excuse me. I asked for two loaves of bread. I'm afraid you've only given me one.

   SHOP ASSISTANT: Oh, I do apologise, sir. Here's the other one – sorry!

4. CUSTOMER: Excuse me, sir. This radio cassette doesn't work. Can you give me a refund for it, please?

   SHOP ASSISTANT: Oh, I'm terribly sorry, we don't give refunds. But maybe we can repair it. Could I see your receipt, please?

Exercise 3

1. Oh, I'm terribly sorry.
2. Oh dear, I didn't mean to! I'm very sorry. Are you OK?
3. I'm terribly sorry, I've been very ill and couldn't phone before.
4. Oh, John, I'm so very sorry! I got the place mixed up. I went to the bus station!
5. I'm sorry. I thought it was for me.
6. I'm so sorry. I thought it was mine.

Exercise 5

I've broken the lid.
He hasn't made the bed
You've got the rug wet.
This glove doesn't fit.
There's a fly in the tin.
It's a quarter past ten!

You didn't scrub the pan!
You didn't buy the pen!
You didn't drive the van!
You didn't pay the men!
You didn't clean my hat!
You didn't feed my pet!

A: I've broken the lid.   B: It's OK. Don't worry!
A: He hasn't made the bed.   B: It's OK. Don't worry!
A: You've got the rug wet.   B: Oh, I'm terribly sorry!
A: This glove doesn't fit.   B: Oh, I'm terribly sorry!
A: There's a fly in the tin.   B: Oh, I'm terribly sorry!
A: It's a quarter past ten!   B: Yes, I'm sorry I'm late.

A: You didn't scrub the pan!   B: I'm very sorry!
A: You didn't buy the pen!   B: I'm sorry!
A: You didn't drive the van!   B: I'm very sorry!
A: You didn't pay the men!   B: I'm sorry!
A: You didn't clean my hat!   B: I'm very sorry!
A: You didn't feed my pet!   B: That's enough, do it yourself!

Exercise 7

I once bought a second-hand car from a used car dealer. It was in wonderful condition – one previous owner, bright red paint, and not many miles on the clock. The car was a bit expensive but the dealer offered me a three months' guarantee. I was still a bit unsure so I asked the dealer to tell me the name of the previous owner. Then I phoned him up and asked lots of questions. Everything seemed OK, so I bought the car; it cost me $9000. At first I was really pleased with the car and went on lots of long journeys – especially when it was hot, because it's best to drive a car a lot when there's only a short guarantee – and then you can find out about other problems. In fact there were no problems. The car was fast, comfortable, quiet ... perfect. Then one day the car made terrible noises and stopped. It needed a new engine. I was angry and phoned the dealer to demand a new engine, but the dealer said he was sorry but the guarantee had finished because I'd bought the car exactly three months and one day before. I was furious but I couldn't do anything. A friend at work reminded me that the Romans had the expression 'Caveat emptor' which in Latin means 'Buyer be careful'. And I said that in this case the Romans would say 'Car-veat emptor' or 'Buyer of car be careful'. He laughed, but as it's cost me an extra $1000 for a new engine, I didn't find it very funny.

UNIT 21 ALL YOU NEED IS LOVE ... OR MONEY

Exercise 5

MAN: What do you need to be happy?

WOMAN: Mm, that's a big question, isn't it?

MAN: Yes *the* big question.

WOMAN: Mm. Well, I'm a pretty easy person to please, really. All I need is nice food, something good to read and someone who loves me.

MAN: Uh huh, but what about money?

WOMAN: Well, personally, I don't need money to be happy, but you need it to live of course.

MAN: And a good job?

WOMAN: I don't think you need a good job to be happy, but you need a job that you like ... a job that feels more like play than work ... Well, that's enough about me, what about you? What do you think you need to be happy?

MAN: Well, you need to be healthy and you need to keep busy, there are so many people who seem unhappy because they don't have enough to do, or don't have enough interests. Luckily my health is good and I'm always busy – that's probably why I seem so happy.

WOMAN: What about a wife?

MAN: Well, I'm not married but I've got lots of friends. I think friends are more important to happiness than wives or husbands.

WOMAN: But what about children?

MAN: I don't think you need children to be happy.

WOMAN: Really?

MAN: Mm ... quite a few of my friends have got children and most of them seem to have quite a few problems, especially those with kids who are about 15 or 16.

WOMAN: My daughter's 14.

MAN: Well, one more year and watch out!

WOMAN: Oh, she's fine, no trouble at all ...

UNIT 22 THE RIGHT CLIMATE?

Exercise 4

What's it like in summer when there are people on the beach? Erm ... it's busy and noisy. I don't like it much.

What do you do when it's hot and the shops are closed? Oh, erm, I go down to the beach and have a swim, or I drive up into the mountains.

Exercise 5

WOMAN: OK, first one ... 'I lie awake at night' is the answer ... What do you think is a suitable question for that one?

MAN: Erm. What do you do if you're ... erm, if you're worried about something?

WOMAN: Mmm. Or: What do you do if you have a big problem?

MAN: Yeah, good. Um, next one ... that's an easy one. What do you do when you don't understand a word?

WOMAN: Oh, yeah, no problem there. Er, what about, ah, what about 'I just relax' ... Mmm ... any ideas?

MAN: What do you do when you go on holiday?

WOMAN: Mmm, that's a good one. I was going to say, 'What do you do if you're on a long flight?'

MAN: Right, next one. Er, where are we? Mmm ... 'I make myself a cup of tea' ... Mmm. What do you ...

WOMAN: What do you do first when you get up in the morning?

MAN: Yeah, right ... and finally ... What do you do ... er, hang on, let's look at the answer again: 'I phone up my friend for a chat'. Why do you phone friends?

WOMAN: Erm, I know: What do you do if you're feeling lonely?

MAN: Oh, yes, of course. That's a good one Well done!

UNIT 23 FESTIVALS

Exercise 1

1. Would you like to come to our house on Saturday? (inviting)
2. Yes, I'd love to. Thanks for asking me. (accepting)
3. Would you like to come to our house on Saturday? (inviting)
4. I'd love to, but I'm afraid I can't. I've got to go to work on Saturday. (declining politely and reason)

Exercise 2

1. WOMAN 1: Would you like to come to my birthday party on Friday?
   WOMAN 2: Yes, I'd love to. What time?
2. MAN: Would you like to come for a meal on Friday evening?
   WOMAN: I can't, I'm afraid, my parents are having a wedding anniversary party.
3. WOMAN 1: Can you come for a coffee this morning?
   WOMAN 2: Yes, great. What time?
4. MAN 1: Would you like to come out for lunch?
   MAN 2: Yes, I would, but I've got too much to do, I'm afraid. Sorry.

Would you like to come to our house on Saturday?
Would you like to come out for lunch?
Can you come for a coffee this morning?
Would you like to come for a meal on Friday evening?

Exercise 3

1. WOMAN: Shall I carry that for you, sir?
   MAN: Oh, yes, thank you. It's very heavy.
2. MAN: Shall I help you with the washing up?
   WOMAN: No, it's OK. I'll do it.
3. WOMAN: Shall we go out to eat tonight?
   MAN: Good idea, there's nothing in here.
4. MAN: Shall I take the dog for a walk?
   WOMAN: Yes, please. I want to finish this book.

Exercise 5

1. I have a special thing that I do on my birthday. I know it's customary to get presents on your birthday, but I always like to send my mother a bunch of flowers on my birthday saying 'Thank you'.
2. In my family we have a special Easter custom, and, er, that is that my parents hide little things in the garden like chocolate eggs and the children then have to … look for them; and we're still doing it although we're all adults.
3. My family and I always eat together on Friday nights, and it's traditional, just for us I think, that the four boys, because I have three brothers, clean the house and clean up afterwards and make coffee and cake or whatever and entertain our parents after dinner.

UNIT 24 LOOKING AHEAD

Exercise 4

1. WOMAN: Will your country have really serious traffic problems in fifteen years from now?
   MAN: Yes, of course, it'll have very serious traffic problems.
2. MAN: Will your country have a new prime minister in ten years from now?
   WOMAN: Yes, I think it will.
3. MAN 1: Will you have more leisure time when you are old?
   MAN 2: Yes, I will. I'll have much more time to do things I enjoy, at least I hope so.
4. WOMAN: Will your country have more tourism in ten years from now?
   MAN: Yes, it will, a lot more.
5. WOMAN 1: Will children need to study harder in the future?
   WOMAN 2: Yes, they will because there will be fewer jobs.
6. MAN: In ten years' time, will your country be a better place to live in?
   WOMAN: No, it won't, it'll be a much worse place to live in. But I hope I'm wrong.
7. WOMAN: Will your English be excellent in ten years' time?
   MAN: Yes, of course it will, it'll be perfect.

Exercise 6

1. What will you do?
   I'll write long letters regularly to lonely Russian electricians.
2. What will they do?
   They'll read your long letters rapidly and correct the spelling errors.

Exercise 7

LYN: Erm, in about ten years from now, do you think people will still write letters, Kate?
KATE: Um, yes, I think they will because people will still be falling in love, and love letters are so much a part of that. Don't, don't you think so?
LYN: Well, I'd like to think so, yes. I think they probably will. I think letters are important.
KATE: Erm, Tris, what about you? Do you think we will still use cash in ten years' time?
TRIS: Ten years down the road? Less and less, I think, because there are places even today that won't accept cash. I was quite shocked to find that in the United States there were places that actually couldn't cope with cash, and after all everybody's got a credit card now.
IAN: What, what about you, Lyn, do you think city life will become more or less pleasant?
LYN: Well, I'm sorry to say I think it will become less pleasant because I can't see people giving up their cars and machinery and all the things that will make pollution much worse than it already is, so I feel a bit negative about that. I think it'll be, I think it'll be quite horrible.

KATE: Um, do you think, Ian, that children will study at home and not at school any more in ten years' time?
IAN: I don't know if they will or not. I don't think so. I feel it's important that children do keep actually going to a place to study, so I hope not, perhaps they will. What about you, Tris, have you got any thoughts on that?
TRIS: Well, I think aside from what you learn at school, the social interaction is really important and you couldn't possibly, I mean if kids stayed at home all the time, they'd never meet other children. I think it would be a ludicrous situation … 'cause, I mean, the most important thing I learned at school was getting on with people.

ANSWER KEY

STARTER UNIT

2 One's the sun, two's the shoe

A

1. sun 2. shoe 3. tree 4. door 5. hive
6. sticks 7. heaven 8. gate 9. line
10. hen

C

4, 7, 9, 12, 15, 18, 23

3 What time is it?

See tapescript for answers.

4 International times

A

1. a quarter past nine in the morning
2. twenty-five to eleven in the morning
3. twenty past eleven in the morning
4. twenty past two in the afternoon
5. twenty-five past four in the afternoon

B

1. 1.25 2. 4.15 3. 11.30 4. 6.15

C

1. six in the evening (6 pm)
2. six in the morning (6 am)
3. eight in the morning (8 am)
4. three in the afternoon (3 pm)
5. eleven in the evening (11 pm)
6. two in the morning (2 am)
7. eleven in the morning (11 am)
8. seven in the evening (7 pm)
9. one in the morning (1 am)
10. four in the morning (4 am)

5 What day is it today?

A

1. Thursday 2. Wednesday 3. Sunday
4. Tuesday 5. June 6. January and October
7. April and July 8. February

6 There are two secretaries in the office

1. teachers 2. actors 3. accountants
4. actresses 5. dictionaries 6. women
7. doctors 8. dentists 9. guesses
10. businessmen 11. crosses 12. parents

7 Is this your office?

A

1. I 2. you 3. you 4. he 5. she
6. we 7. they

B

2. our 4. his 6. her 8. their 9. your
10. my

8 Where's the phone?

1. It's on the table, by the window. (A)
2. It's on the floor, under the table. (B)
3. It's on the desk in the classroom, beside the door. (B)
4. They're on the chair, next to the desk. (B)
5. They're in the bedroom, on the shelf over the bed. (A)
6. They're on the table, next to the lamp. (A)
7. It's opposite the door. (B)

1 FINDING OUT

1 What's the long form?

1. name is 2. Where is 3. It is 4. I am
5. He is 6. She is 7. We are 8. They are
9. is not 10. are not

2 What's your name?

1. Are you Maria?
2. Are you a journalist?
3. Where are you from?
4. What's your address?
5. Where's the painting?
6. Is there a coffee shop? *or* Is there a coffee shop in this building?
7. Are there any public telephones?

4 Words that go together

A

1. coffee shop 2. public telephones
3. first floor 4. parking spaces
5. information desk 6. natural light

B

1. a radio; a television; a chair; a table; a window; a computer
2. a chair; a table; a window; a computer; public telephones
3. a radio; a television; a chair; a table; a window; a lift; stairs; an information desk; public telephones; a coffee shop; a computer
4. public telephones; a coffee shop; parking spaces (sometimes: an information desk)

5 She's a waitress

1. teacher 2. doctor 3. dentist 4. lawyer
5. electrician 6. plumber 7. mechanic
8. cleaner 9. businessman 10. businesswoman
11. flight attendants

6 Numbers

See tapescript for answers.

7 Directory enquiries

A

Dominica 1809, Finland 358, Thailand 66

B

1. Darby, 26 Rutland Avenue, Oxford, 4878761
2. Wrightson, 42 Main Street, Minneapolis, 695 7309
3. MacTavish, Burns House, Dixon Road, Edinburgh 031 566 2389

8 Where do you come from?

1. Arturo   2. Chile   3. Patel
4. India, from the northern part of India   5. Philip
6. the United States   7. the United States

10 English teacher required

A

1. teacher   2. teacher   3. gardener, translator
4. gardener   5. translator   6. gardener

11 Visual dictionary

1. secretary   2. cafeteria   3. window
4. television   5. lift   6. cleaner   7. stairs
8. library   9. dentist

2 WHAT HAVE YOU GOT?

1 I've got a dictionary

B

1. 1   2. 1   3. 2   4. 0   5. 1   6. 0
7. 0   8. 4   9. 0; but the library's got 2

2 To have

2. You have got – You've got   3. He has got
4. She's got   5. It has got – It's got
6. We have got – We've got
7. They have got – They've got

3 Have you got any plants?

1. any friends   2. a pen friend; some cousins
3. a pen   4. a computer; a notebook; some
newspapers; some pens; a pencil   5. any plants
6. any at all; some plants

4 Mary and John have got two sons

1. Michael   2. Mary and John   3. Paul; Susan
4. Joy   5. Paul   6. Susan   7. Michael
8. Mary and John   9. Paul; James

6 I've got a brother and two sisters

A

men: husband; son; brother; father
women: sister; daughter; mother; wife
men or women: parent; grandparent; cousin; friend

B

a. 2   b. 4   c. 1   d. 3

7 What have you got in your pocket?

B

Speaker 1: 1. money   2. string
   3. a packet of biscuits   4. glasses   5. house key
   6. car keys   7. paper handkerchiefs
Speaker 2: 1. dirty tissue   2. car keys   3. money
   4. a piece of chewing gum

C

1. piece   2. paper   3. nothing; hole   4. dirty

8 My bedroom

B

1. c   2. b   3. a

9 House swap

Possible questions:
How many beds has it got?
Is there a parking space for the car?
Has it got a big sitting room?
Has it got a bath or a shower?
Have you got any plants?

10 Visual dictionary

1. table   2. pen   3. money   4. car keys
5. comb

3 WHAT WOULD YOU LIKE TO EAT?

1 One packet of rice

1. cartons   2. tins   3. box   4. bottles
5. egg   6. apple   7. potato   8. tomatoes
9. carrot   10. chocolate

2 I'd like four bananas, please

A

Countable nouns: apple; banana; bean; pea; grape;
   biscuit; bottle; orange
Uncountable nouns: sugar; rice; water; milk; spaghetti;
   money; wine; cheese; noodles; chocolate; toast; cake;
   cereal; butter; lamb; beef; yoghurt; fruit juice; bread;
   soup

Note: Some nouns are used as both countables and
uncountables; e.g. *cake* can mean one large cake cut into
slices (uncountable). For this, use: 'Would you like some
(or a piece of) cake?' and 'I'd like some cake, please.'
Cake can also mean several individual cakes on a plate
(countable). For this, use: 'Would you like a cake (or:
one of these cakes?)' and 'I'd like a cake, please.' ('I'd like
two cakes, please').

B

1. some   2. uncountable; some

3 Milk comes in bottles

A

1. bananas   2. potatoes   3. eggs   4. carrots
5. lettuce   6. apples

C

1. rice; noodles; pasta   2. milk and fruit juice
3. meat   4. vegetables and fruit   5. milk; wine
6. spaghetti and noodles   7. eggs   8. milk; soup
9. milk   10. soup   11. apples; oranges; beans and
other vegetables / fruit and vegetables   12. apples;
oranges; beans and other vegetables / fruit and
vegetables

4 Shoppers' mistakes

See tapescript for possible answers.

5 Stress and intonation

B

See tapescript for answers.

C

1. b   2. b   3. b   4. b

6 How much is this?

B

1. this   2. these   3. those   4. that   5. this
6. this   7. those   8. those   9. that

C

pineapple, bananas, mineral water, orange juice,
tomatoes, cheese

7 I like Indian food

A

5, 1, 3, 8, 13, 12, 9

8 Changing diets

B

1. b   2. a   3. b

D

breads; cakes and biscuits; snack foods; tinned goods;
fizzy soft drinks; pasta; breakfast cereals; butter; cheese;
lamb; beef; milk drinks; fresh milk; flavoured long-life
milk; yoghurts

9 Visual dictionary

1. lettuce   2. bananas   3. carrots
4. pineapple   5. grapes   6. chicken
7. salmon   8. sardines   9. ice cream
10. bread rolls   11. milk   12. noodles

4 A SENSE OF COLOUR

2 Where does he buy his socks?

1. c. buys   2. f. buys   3. j. buy   4. h. buy
5. b. buy   6. i. buy   7. e. gives   8. g. receives
9. a. buy   10. d. sings

3 Brown or black shoes?

C

See tapescript for answers.

4 There's a grey cloud in the sky!

1. pink   2. black   3. orange   4. grey
5. blue   6. brown   7. red   8. gold
9. green   10. yellow

5 Fashionable, conventional or comfortable?

A

1. c   2. a   3. l   4. k   5. q   6. b
7. e   8. r   9. d   10. i   11. h   12. g
13. n   14. m   15. f   16. o   17. j   18. p

C

Woman: 1. green, red   2. a   3. c   4. a
              5. a and b
Man: 1. checks, blues   2. a   3. c
           4. b   5. b

6 Consonants at the beginning of words

A

See tapescript for answers.

7 The colours of my country

B

First speaker: a. dark green; earth colours
    b. many different colours
    c. red, white and blue
    d. ——
Second speaker: a. Before the monsoon: brown, red.
    After the monsoon: green
    b. many colours, reds, blues, orange, purple, yellow
    c. red, green, orange, white
    d. white
The first speaker is from the USA.
The second speaker is from Malaysia.

8 Jeans give self-confidence

A

1. denim (cotton)   2. the USA

C

1. b   2. a   3. a   4. b   5. b

10 Visual dictionary

1. tie   2. sweater   3. boots   4. gloves
5. skirt   6. sandals   7. T-shirt   8. shorts

5 GOOD HABITS, NEW ROUTINES?

1 Why does he go shopping in the market?

A

See tapescript for answers.

B

See tapescript for possible answers.

2 Words that go together

get dressed   tidy the kitchen
have some coffee   read a book
listen to music   wash the dishes
have a shower   go shopping
go to bed   make the bed
watch TV

3 I always look, and she always listens

2. s   3. es   4. have   5. has

6 Do you read travel books?

B

1. a   2. b   3. b   4. b   5. a   6. a

C

1. d   2. b   3. c   4. e   5. a
6. Because it's not good for you.

7 He finds murderers!

B

a. murderer   b. the ceiling
c. a medical examiner   d. a rubbish bin
e. a body

D

1. h   2. e   3. b   4. d   5. f   6. a
7. g   8. c

8 International Video Club

1. c   2. b   3. d   4. a

9 Visual dictionary

1. He cleans his teeth.   2. She gets up.
3. He has a shower.   4. She has a cup of coffee.
5. She reads the paper.   6. He watches television.
7. She comes home.

6 THE WAY YOU LOOK

1 Beautiful eyes

A

1. noun   2. before

B

1. An <u>artistic</u> person is usually <u>lively</u>.
2. Her <u>young</u> sister has an <u>intelligent</u> face.
3. A smile is very <u>important</u> at interviews.
4. Juanita is a <u>proud</u> mother.
5. An <u>ambitious</u> secretary is <u>serious</u>.
6. Our friend has a <u>happy</u> personality.

3 He is kind, and his kindness is important to me

A

1. kindness   2. sad   3. seriousness   4. selfish
5. liveliness   6. happy   7. friendly
8. intelligence   9. confident   10. beautiful
11. health

B

1. a   2. b   3. a   4. b   5. a; b   6. a; b

4 Vowel sounds and sentence rhythms

A

1. hand; bag; man; jacket; back
2. legs; chest; neck; men

B

See tapescript for answers.

C

See tapescript for answers.

5 Appearance is important

B

1. eyes; clean hair
2. smile; happy face; a smile in your eyes

6 An appearance that shows emotion

C

Answers for the seven sentences:
1. No   2. Yes   3. Yes   4. No   5. Yes
6. No   7. Yes
Qualities of models:
    a. intelligent; lively; beautiful; lots of personality
    b. an appearance that speaks, that shows emotion;
    intelligence; beautiful, strong women

D

Possible ending: the photographers are getting old, and
they don't like to compare themselves with their young
models.

7 A job application

A

The words in order:
I am; speak English; am; intelligent; lively; happy

9 Visual dictionary

1. ear   2. nose   3. leg   4. hand   5. lively
6. selfish   7. shy   8. artistic

7 WHAT CAN WE DO?

1 I can't, I really can't

1. write
2. can't; cannot; Can
3. can't wait; cannot wait; Can she wait?
4. He can't play; He cannot play; Can he play?
5. We can't read; We cannot read; Can we read?
6. They can't type; They cannot type; Can they type?

2 Could you pass the milk, please?

1. Can you (*or* Could you) lend me your book, please?
2. Can you (*or* Could you) get me a cup of tea, please?
3. Can you wait a minute? (informal) Could you wait a
    minute, please? (formal)
4. Can you be quiet and listen? (impatient) *or* Could you
    be quiet and listen, please? (patient)
5. Can you (*or* Could you) write it on the board, please?
6. Can you (*or* Could you) show me where to sign,
    please?
7. Can you (*or* Could you) tell me where the bank is,
    please?

3 Now and then

A

1. T   2. N   3. T   4. T   5. N   6. N
7. N   8. N   9. T   10. N   11. T
12. N   13. N   14. N

4 I went to school every day

1. b. went   2. b. went   3. a. go   4. b. was
5. a. are   6. b. was   7. a. are   8. b. were
10. a. have   10. b. had   11. b. had
12. a. have   12. b. had   14. a. can
15. b. could   16. a. can   16. b. could

5 I can play the drums

A

1. *Possible answers:* a photocopier; a computer; some machines
2. a meal
3. poems; a number; a meal; stories; a letter; important dates
4. poems; stories; a letter; a number
5. the drums; the guitar; the piano
6. poems; a number; stories; a letter; important dates
7. my clothes
8. a car; a photocopier; a computer; some machines
9. a car
10. a bank account; a letter

B

PROFILE

0–10 ticks: You can do some things, but there is still a lot for you to learn. Try learning one new skill this year.

10–20 ticks: You have a lot of skills. There are many things you can do. Look at the things you have not ticked. Is there anything useful you can learn? Skills are very important in the modern world.

20+ ticks: Are you telling the truth? You really have a lot of skills! There are a lot of things you can do. Can you now teach others these important skills for survival in the modern world?

6 We can play the piano with two fingers!

1. on   2. in (*or* on)   3. in   4. at   5. with
6. at   7. to; to   8. to   9. to   10. at
11. on   12. in

7 Weak forms

B

1. <u>Can</u> you read in a car? No, I can't, I get sick.
2. <u>Can</u> you type? Yes, I can. I <u>can</u> type very quickly, with two fingers.
3. <u>Can</u> you cook a good meal? Yes, I can. I <u>can</u> do it in twenty minutes.
4. <u>Can</u> you write a poem? No, I can't. I can't think of rhymes.
5. <u>Can</u> you stand on your head? Yes, of course I can. I <u>can</u> stand on my head for five minutes.
6. <u>Can</u> you drive a car? Well, of course I can. I <u>can</u> even fly a plane.

8 Are you feeling all right, son?

A

See tapescript for answers.

C

Possible answers:
1. his mother
2. he only has three A's (*or* his marks are not good enough)
3. have a good life in the future
4. he can pass easily

10 Visual dictionary

2. He can type.   3. She can use a computer.
5. He can iron clothes.   6. She can cook.
7. He can play the guitar and she can play the drums.
8. He can write a letter.   9. She can drive a car.
10. They can walk to school by themselves.
11. They can go to work by bus.
12. He can stand on his head.

8 LOVE IT OR HATE IT!

2 Pollution is a problem in our city

A

Facilities: shops; parks; cinemas; markets; restaurants; bridges
Possible problems: pollution; noise; traffic; crowds; prices

B

Words that could be added:
Facilities: open spaces; woodlands; streets; public transport
Possible problems: heat; cold; tourists

3 How many legs have spiders got?

A

1. tails: snake; dog; cat; goat; horse; rat; fish
2. four legs: dog; cat; goat; horse; rat
3. six legs: mosquito; fly; cockroach

4 The vowel sounds in *dog* and *goat*

A

See tapescript for answers.

B

Words that have vowel sounds like *dog*: frog; log; dog; fog; the first vowel in mosquito
Words with vowel sounds like *goat*: goat; boat; hippo; disco; the last vowel in mosquito; toe; show; go; home

6 I usually take the children swimming

A

1. to sleep in; works; goes; generally
2. takes; watch television; market
3. usually; goes; gets; has
4. does; like; takes; likes to have; buys

B

1. washing up; bus
2. driving; doing the washing
3. spiders
4. spiders; cockroaches

7 Expatriates

A

The text says that successful expatriates are those who get a lot of pleasure from living in a different culture; curious; adventurous; cheerful, positive; enthusiastic; healthy
They like meeting new people
They love travel for itself; new experiences; trying new and exotic food

8 Yes, I love travelling

A

Gertrude: 2. you see things more clearly, you notice more things   4. yes   5. yes   6. no
Jean-Pierre: 1. yes   3. yes   4. yes   6. no

B

1. They get a lot of pleasure from living in a different culture; they are cheerful, they love travel and trying new and exotic food.
2. They don't read about the new country.

9 Welcome to South Australia

B

interesting stores; a major shopping centre; restaurants; parks; gardens; discos; pubs; piano bars; cabarets; the famous Adelaide Casino; excellent museums

11 Visual dictionary

1. cat   2. dog   3. goat   4. horse   5. rat
6. snake   7. fish   8. spider   9. fly

9 THOSE WERE THE DAYS

1 Was your life happy?

A

1. were   2. were   3. Was   4. were
5. Were   6. Was   7. Was   8. was
9. Were   10. Was   11. Was   12 Were
13. did   14. Did   15. Did   16. Did
17. Did   18. did   19. did; get   20. did

B

1. When were you born?
2. When you were a child, where did you live?
3. Where did you go to school?
4. When did you get married?
5. Was your life happy? or Were you happy?
6. How many children did you have? or Did you have any children?

2 I phoned them from home

A

He lived with *her* until 1985, when he got married. At first he stayed in the same town with his wife and mother, but later he moved with *them* to New York. He loved the big city so much that he mentioned *it* in one of his newspaper articles. So one day he telephoned Tom and asked *him* to take the next plane to New York. He now had a lovely wife and two daughters, and he wanted to stay in New Zealand with *them*.

B

1. her   2. him   3. her   4. it   5. them

3 My life story

1. I *was* born in England, but my parents *were/are* not English. My father *was/is* from Poland, and my mother *was/is* Russian. I *went* to school in Bournemouth, where my father *was/is* a dentist. When I *finished* school, I *decided* to travel.
2. I *went* to Russia to see my grandmother. But on the way I *visited* Rome, and there I *went* to a dentist. He was wonderful! Like my father! I *got married* and *stayed* in Italy. I *had* two children.
3. Then we *moved* to Bucharest. When we *arrived*, I didn't know anybody. I *was* lonely. So I *decided* to be a teacher. I *was* very good at English, of course, so I *started* to teach English. Now we live in Germany. I still teach English, but now I teach at the university.

4 I started a new job yesterday

A

1. d   2. b   3. e   4. f   5. c   6. a
Eighteen verbs in the past tense: started; asked; stayed; wanted; refused; sacked; tried; phoned; walked; laughed; hated; played; arrived; thanked; called; looked; seemed; smiled

B

1. asked; sacked; walked; laughed; thanked; looked
2. started; wanted; hated
3. stayed; refused; tried; phoned; played; arrived; called; seemed; smiled

6 The shark

A

1. c   2. f   3. d   4. e   5. g   6. b
7. h   8. i   9. a

C

1. b   2. a   3. b   4. c   5. a   6. c
7. b

D

See tapescript for answers.

7 Little arguments

C

See tapescript for answers.

8 Visual dictionary

1. lived   2. stayed   3. went   4. arrived
5. was   6. liked   7. was   8. played

10 ONCE UPON A TIME

1 I didn't go to work last week because I was ill

B

Possible questions:
1. Did you forget about our meeting?
2. Did you go to the cinema last week?
3. What did you see?
4. Did you speak to the manager?
5. What did she tell you?

2 She caught a train to Valencia

A

with my feet: I went; I came; I ran
with my hands: I caught; I wrote
with my mouth: I ate; I said; I spoke; I told
with my ears: I heard
with my eyes: I saw; I read

B

1. a train; a sound; some music; a small child; a scream; a shot
2. a train; a ball; an apple; a fish
3. a meal; an apple; a fish
4. a book; a train; a painting; a ball; an apple; a small child; a newspaper; a little cottage; a light; a fish
5. a book; a newspaper

3 Last week I went to the theatre

1. met a friend; went to the theatre.
2. musical.
3. got up and left; forgot about her umbrella under the seat.
4. found a café; sat outside.
5. a coffee; a sandwich.
6. began to rain.
7. ran back to the theatre.
8. had her umbrella.

4 Rhythm rap

A

caught; forgot; was; sat; fed; do

5 How did the world begin?

A

1. The first sunrise: 1. e   2. g   3. d
   How the birds made the world: 1. c   2. a
   3. f   4. b
2. See tapescript for answers.

B

1. T   2. F   3. T   4. F   5. T   6. F
7. T   8. F   9. F

6 Dinosaurs

A

1. f   2. b   3. d   4. e   5. g   6. c
7. a

C

See tapescript for answers.

7 An accident

1. Date of accident: *Monday, 9th October*
2. Time of accident: *10 am*
3. Place of accident: *Near the market, on the corner of Market Street and Main Street.*
4. Description of the accident: *A car went round the corner and straight into a fruit stand. The stand shattered and the car hit Ms. F. Alonzo and knocked her to the ground.*

8 Visual dictionary

1. met   3. said   5. ate   8. saw   9. went
11. sat   12. told   14. rang   15. ran
16. caught

11 WHAT'S GOING ON?

2 What are you doing? I'm studying English

A

6. What's he learning?
7. What is she learning? What's she learning?
8. What are they learning? / What're they learning?

B

1. are you   4. watching
2. are; reading   5. are; They're going
3. What's; She's   6. are; We're

C

1. having   2. listening   3. making
4. writing   5. living   6. getting   7. running

3 Paintings from different centuries

Possible descriptions:
1. In painting a, there is a group of people on a beach. They are camping. A fire is burning. There are some fish nearby. Two people are sitting and talking in a little hut made from some trees. Three men are sitting on the beach. One man is lying on his stomach. A young boy is standing. He's holding a spear. There are also two dogs. They're sitting beside the men.
2. In painting b, there are many people on a beach. There is a bridge with several people on it. A man, a woman and a girl are standing still on the bridge. Another woman is walking. In front of the bridge, there are three people. One woman is wearing a hat with a feather. She's sitting in a chair and reading a newspaper. One man is standing by the water, looking out to sea. Another man is lying on the beach. He's probably asleep. Behind the bridge, an older man is walking with a lady. She's carrying an

umbrella or parasol. The man's looking back, perhaps looking at the people on the bridge. Further away, behind the bridge, many people are walking on the beach. A woman is holding a small girl by the hand.

4 We're watching TV

1. a cake; a cup of tea; a party; a meal; a shower
2. a table; a new house
3. the news; the radio; English; me; music; his friend; a question; a new language
4. English; the present continuous tense; a new language
5. the news; a film; television; football
6. the news; a book; English; the present continuous tense; a question; a new language
7. a cake; a table; a film; a cup of tea; a new house; a meal
8. Spain; Tokyo
9. the telephone; the doorbell; me; a question
10. me; his friend; a taxi

5 News reports from the past

A

1. c   2. b   3. a

B

The reporter is standing in the central square. There is *thick smoke* everywhere. Lava *is beginning* to pour down the mountain. People *are packing up* everything they can and *leaving* the city. The roads are full of people *trying to* get away.
The whole city *is waiting* for the President's car. There are many people *waiting* by the side of the road, some waving flags. The President *is sitting* in the back seat beside the First Lady. They're both *smiling* and *waving* to the crowds. There is a shot. The President is slumping forwards.
The reporter is on the beach. There is a big white monster on the water. A boat *is leaving* the monster and is coming over the water. Many people *are waiting* on the beach. Some *are waving* their hands and some *are shouting*. Strange people are in the boat. They *are* wearing very strange coloured clothes and their skin is very *white*. And now, they're *getting out* of the boat, and coming onto the beach. The people *are moving* back in fear …

6 What are teenagers reading?

A

1. f   2. e   3. b   4. c   5. a   6. d

D

1. listening to music or watching television; are reading for pleasure every week.
2. buying; 11; reading a lot of magazines
3. buying a variety of magazines, many of them about health and fitness, the environment, popular science
4. videos, films and going out!

7 A DIY card

Possible additions to the card:
I am feeling *rather sick*
I am *working as usual*; *doing my routine as usual*; *not working very hard*
I am having *a hard time*; *a difficult time*; *a lot of fun*; *a boring time*; *an interesting time*
I am *waiting for a letter from you*; *tired of waiting for a letter from you*; *going on a holiday*; *tired of life*; *happy without you*
I hope you are *lonely for me*; *missing me*; *sad without me*; *making a lot of money*; *being good*
Other possible greetings: *Love and kisses*; *See you soon*; *Write soon*

8 Visual dictionary

2. drinking   3. eating   4. talking   5. dancing
6. answering   7. arriving   8. cooking
9. making   12. reading   13. watching
14. building

12 MAKING PLANS

1 After work she's meeting a friend

2. he's; he's going to
3. taking; she's
4. seeing (*or* meeting); flying
5. they're; having; restaurant
6. he's talking on the telephone, but after work he's playing
7. writing; after work, she's going to the dentist

2 We're going to the restaurant on Monday evening

B

1. We're going shopping *on* Friday.
2. Are you going to your English class *tonight*?
3. The manager *is flying* to Belgium in December.
4. Don't forget: the meeting is *at* 9 o'clock.
5. We always take our holidays *in* the winter.
6. Are you visiting a friend *this weekend*?
7. *They're* not playing tennis on Saturday afternoon.
8. We're meeting them at 3 o'clock *on* Monday morning.

3 We're going on holiday!

1. We're going to a: party; cinema; picnic; market
2. We're going to the: party; cinema; shops; school; picnic; market
3. We're going to: play football; work; school; play tennis; bed
4. We're going out with: my family; the children
5. We're going on a: bus; drive; holiday; boat
6. We're going in a: bus; boat

4 *-ing* sounds and sentence rhythm

A

1. cake   2. book   3. hat   4. beach
5. game

5 Where are you going on holiday?

A

1. d 　 2. f 　 3. e 　 4. a 　 5. c 　 6. b

C

1. Cliff Michelmore
2. Peter Middleton
3. Mike Smith
4. Eamonn Fahey
5. Peter Middleton
6. Caroline Dawney
7. Anne Winterton
8. Eamonn Fahey

7 Visual dictionary

2. have a birthday party 　 3. move to a new town
4. going to change my job
5. going to paint the kitchen
6. going to do some gardening
7. go on holiday by the sea 　 8. learn to drive a car
9. I'm going to get married 　 10. to visit my parents
11. going to buy a new car
12. we're going to go skiing

13 BETTER AND BETTER

1 Comparing countries

1. bigger 　 2. is smaller 　 3. are higher
4. is longer 　 5. is larger 　 6–12 answers will vary

2 I'm older than my brother

1. F 　 2. T 　 3. T 　 4. T 　 5. F

4 Good or bad?

for people:
usually good: outgoing; friendship; slim; optimistic
good and bad: reserved

for countries or cities:
usually good: atmosphere
usually bad: polluted; crowded
good and bad: cheap

for countries, cities or people:
usually good: lively; tidy; exciting
usually bad: noisy

The two nouns are: *friendship* and *atmosphere*.

5 Comparing pictures

6 Shall I compare you to ...

See tapescript for answers.

7 I like this one best!

1. c; b; a
2. b; a; c
3. a; c; b
4. b; c; a

8 English sayings

1. A chain is only as strong as its weakest link. f
2. The best things in life are free. g
3. Least said soonest mended. b
4. The sooner the better. h
5. The best kind of advice is no advice at all. e
6. The first step is always the hardest. c
7. The worst may never happen. a
8. An empty vessel makes the biggest sound. d

10 Visual dictionary

1. Paris 　 2. France 　 3. Portugal 　 4. Lisbon
5. Italy 　 6. Rome 　 7. Turkey 　 8. Ankara
9. India 　 10. New Delhi 　 11. Japan
12. Tokyo 　 13. Thailand 　 14. Bangkok
15. Indonesia 　 16. Jakarta 　 17. Canada
18. Ottawa 　 19. Mexico 　 20. Mexico City
21. Chile 　 22. Santiago 　 23. Brazil
24. Brasilia

14 A SPIRIT OF ADVENTURE

1 I've started

I've started.
You've started.
He/she/it's started.
We've started.
They've started.

I haven't started.
You haven't started.
She/he/it hasn't started.
We haven't started.
They haven't started.

Have you finished?
Has she/he/it finished?
Have they/we finished?

2 The taxi's arrived

See tapescript for answers.

It's stopped raining is the short form of *It has stopped raining.*

3 Have you ever slept all night on a beach?

See tapescript for answers.

5 Sports

Sports with a ball: golf; soccer; tennis; cricket; basketball
Water sports: scuba diving; sailing
Sports in the air: skydiving; ballooning
Other sports: karate; horse riding; ice hockey; motor
　 racing

6 I haven't had time

Have you **done** your **home**work?
I'm **sorry** but I haven't had **time**.

7 She's suffering from stress

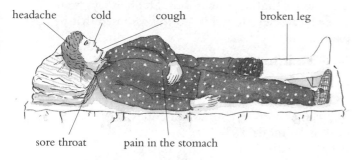

headache   cold   cough   broken leg

sore throat   pain in the stomach

Patient 1: He's got a pain in his back.
Patient 2: She's got a sore throat.
Patient 3: She feels tired and stressed.

8 Have you ever seen sumo wrestling?

	Man	
	Has he been to / seen it? Yes/No	Did he enjoy it? Yes/No / Yes and no
soccer		
cricket		
horse racing	Yes	Yes and no
skiing	Yes	Yes
sumo wrestling	Yes	Yes
	Woman	
	Has she been to / seen it? Yes/No	Did she enjoy it? Yes/No / Yes and no
soccer	No	–
cricket	Yes	Yes
horse racing		
skiing	Yes	Yes
sumo wrestling	Yes	No

9 Progress reports

1. Pehr has made good progress in grammar, speaking (and listening).
2. He has had a few problems with some expressions, verb tenses, intonation and homework.
3. He has tried to improve his writing.
4. He hasn't worked very hard on his reading.

11 Visual dictionary

1. archery   2. basketball   3. cricket
4. fishing   5. horse racing   6. karate
7. motor racing   8. volleyball   9. swimming
10. tennis

15 DOES BEING TIDY SAVE TIME?

1 Questions and answers
See tapescript for answers.

3 Before going to sleep
Speaker 1: Question 2
Speaker 2: Question 7
Speaker 3: Question 1
Speaker 4: Question 5

4 Companies always want people with experience

Finding a job is not easy these days. *Writing* hundreds of letters and *making* hundreds of phone calls just doesn't seem to be enough. Companies always want people with experience, but you can't get experience without a job. *Putting* all those 'Thanks, but no, thanks' replies into the bin is not pleasant and *buying* newspapers every day is expensive. *Going to* interviews is interesting, but it makes me sad when another person always gets the job.

5 You put waste paper in the bin
computer – disk
diary – appointment
desk – office chair
bin – waste paper
photocopier – sheets of paper
mug – coffee

6 They're handy for standing on
Old business cards are handy for:
1. writing notes
2. putting a drink on
3. planning a talk (you write notes on them)

An old mug is handy for:
1. storing things like pens, pencils, paper clips
2. keeping rubber bands

Old telephone books are useful for:
1. putting computers on
2. standing on
3. keeping the door open

7 Infomania
B
1. Put everything unimportant on a desk and everything important on the floor.
   Put papers into bags and then write the date on each bag. The bags go to the garden shed or the garage. Throw a bag away if you haven't opened it by the end of six months.
2. The writer's answer is probably *no*.
C
1. unimportant   2. worse   3. to ignore
D
1. The problem is there is just so much information these days that it's impossible really to know very much at all.
2. The more choice we have, the more anxious we seem to be about making bad decisions.

9 Visual dictionary

1. facsimile machine   2. calendar   3. bin
4. photocopier   5. filing cabinet   6. in-tray
7. computer   8. keyboard   9. disk
10. envelopes   11. letters   12. calculator
13. desk   14. telephone   15. office chair

16 OUR NEIGHBOURHOOD

1 *I saw, I've seen*

I've gone; to see; I've eaten; I took; I made; to do; I found; I've had; I bought; I've bought

2 I've just packed my suitcase

1. I've just checked my ticket and passport.
2. I've just written/finished a letter to John.
3. I've just washed my hair.
4. I've just phoned for a taxi.

3 No, not yet

a. Has Elena seen (*Jurassic Park*) yet?
b. Has your brother phoned (Harrods) yet?
c. Have Carlos and Miguel bought (an alarm clock) yet?
d. Have you read (the *Washington Post*) yet?

4 A watch is a thing

A

1. f   2. e   3. c   4. b   5. a   6. d

B

1. A cousin is a person who is your aunt's child.
2. A department store/supermarket/hypermarket is a place where you can buy almost anything.
3. A daily newspaper is a thing that people read in the morning and throw away at night.

6 It's the petrol station

A

1. the library
2. the petrol station
3. the tourist office
4. the railway station
5. the shopping centre

B

See tapescript for answers.

7 Just the headlines

	paper	bank	shopping	holiday	bill
Jackie:	No	Yes	No	No	**Yes**
Stephen:	Yes	**Yes**	Yes	Yes	Yes
Dave:	Yes	No	No	**Yes**	No

Mike's questions:
Have you read the paper yet today?
Have you been to the bank yet today, or this week?
Have you done the shopping yet this week?
Have you had a holiday yet this year?
Have you paid an electricity bill yet this year?

Note:
The tape is slightly ambiguous. Stephen says he has received an electricity bill, so it is assumed that he has paid it.

8 Give it to charity?

A

They're fun. ☑
You can end up buying stolen goods. ☑
You make money. ☑
People are giving less to charities. ☑
There are legal problems. ☑
They're helpful in hard times. ☑
People are becoming too selfish. ☑
You learn about selling. ☑
You can't get your money back easily. ☑

B

1. f   2. c   3. e   4. d   5. a   6. b

9 For Sale

Vehicles: Toyota Corolla hatchback
Electronic equipment: JVC stereo system; IBM compatible
Clothes: wedding dress; leather jacket
Animals: baby rabbits; Anglo Arab mare
Musical instruments: guitar

10 Visual dictionary

1. shopping centre   2. car park   3. hospital
4. park   5. airport   6. railway station
7. church   8. university   9. petrol station
10. library   11. town hall   12. tourist office
13. post office   14. bank   15. factory

17 IT'S WORTH DOING WELL

1 Thinking about adverbs and adjectives

Possible answers:
1. Adjectives are used with nouns. Examples: a good book, a *slow train*.
2. Adverbs are used with *verbs*. Examples: She eats quickly, He drinks *noisily*.
3. To form many adverbs, add *-ly* to the adjective. Examples: complete – completely, *different – differently*.
4. Some adverbs are different. Example: good – *well*.

4 Opposites

Adjective	Opposite	Adverb	Opposite
tidy	untidy	tidily	**untidily**
good	bad	**well**	**badly**
quick	slow	quickly	**slowly**
skilful	clumsy	**skilfully**	**clumsily**
patient	**impatient**	**patiently**	impatiently
careful	careless	carefully	**carelessly**
noisy	**quiet**	**noisily**	quietly
natural	unnatural	**naturally**	**unnaturally**

5 Describe a good language learner

The things mentioned are 1, 2, 4, 5 and 6.

6 Using a video camera

A

The topics mentioned in the text are 1, 2, 3 and 4.

B

1. S   2. S   3. D   4. S   5. S   6. D

C

Only number 4 (photograph) is not used.

8 Visual dictionary

1. pottery   2. gardening   3. stamp collecting
4. photography   5. origami   6. jewellery making
7. wood carving   8. cooking   9. camping

18 ON YOUR TRAVELS

1 You should stop at stop signs

2. You shouldn't smoke.
3. You should fasten your seat belt.
4. You should put litter in the bin.
   or You shouldn't drop litter.
5. You shouldn't park your car for more than half an hour.
   or You should only park for half an hour.
6. You should turn right to get/claim your baggage.
7. You should go straight ahead for something to eat or drink.
8. You should wash this (article of clothing) in warm water.
9. You shouldn't iron this (article of clothing).

2 I have to catch the train

1. O   I have to get a visa.
2. G   You should go to gate 3.
3. NO   He doesn't have to drink bottled water.
4. O   She has to catch the train.
5. NO   We don't have to show our passports.
6. G   They shouldn't forget their tickets.

3 Should I carry cash?

1. Which gate should passengers go to?
2. Where should travellers apply for visas / a visa?
3. When should she get a/her visa?
4. What kind of water should I/we drink?
5. Do we have to have a visa?
6. Does he have to have a return ticket?
7. Do we all have to go through Customs?
8. What does she have to fill in?
   or What should she fill in?
9. Where do I have to sign?
   or Where should I sign?
   or Where do I sign?
10. Can I change my seat, please?
    or Can I move to a different seat, please?

4 The travel agent's special offer

See tapescript for answers.

5 Go to the information desk

Go to	Go to the
Egypt	embassy
South America	station
São Paulo	United States
gate 7	travel agency
work	check-in counter
school	Middle East
Tokyo	exit
bed	hotel
platform number 8	duty-free shop

6 Fill in the form

PLEASE PRINT			
1. FAMILY NAME	SPENCER		
2. CHRISTIAN OR GIVEN NAMES	WILLIAM		
3. COUNTRY OF CITIZENSHIP	BRITAIN	4. PASSPORT NUMBER	532675E
5. COUNTRY OF BIRTH	SINGAPORE	6. DATE OF BIRTH	Day 17 / Month 8 / Year 73
7. SEX Male ☑ Female ☐	8. MARITAL STATUS Never Married ☑ Now Married ☐		Widowed ☐ Divorced ☐

9. Please answer ONE of **D** or **E** or **F**

D Visitor or temporary entrant departing
1. I have been in Australia this visit for a period of
Years
Months
OR
Days
2. In Australia I spent most time in
(State or City)
3. Country of residence

E Resident departing temporarily
1. I intend to stay abroad for a period of
Years / Months **1** OR Days
2. Main reason for going abroad (Please mark ONLY ONE box)
Student vacation ☐ 1   Visiting relatives ☑ 5
Convention ☐ 2   Holiday ☐ 6
Business ☐ 3   Employment ☐ 7
Accompanying business traveller ☐ 4   Education ☐ 8   Other ☐ 9
3. Country in which I shall spend most time PORTUGAL
4. In Australia I live in SYDNEY
(State or Territory)

F Resident departing permanently
INCLUDES persons who came to settle in Australia
1. Country of future residence
2. In Australia I lived in
(State or Territory)
3. If not born in Australia how long ago did you come to live in Australia?
Years / Months
4. Did you intend to SETTLE permanently?
Yes ☐   No ☐

10. USUAL OCCUPATION	CHEF	
11. DEPARTURE DETAILS Date 12 / 7 / day month year	Flight No./ Name of Ship BA 009	Airport/ Port SYDNEY
12. COUNTRY IN WHICH I SHALL GET OFF THIS FLIGHT OR SHIP (ABROAD) BRITAIN	SIGNATURE	/ / 19

7 Health care for travellers

1. F   2. F   3. T   4. T   5. F   6. T
7. F   8. T   9. F   10. T

8 Travellers should use insect repellent

Travellers have to …
– have injections against yellow fever for some countries.
– take anti-malarial tablets regularly.

Travellers don't have to …
– have as many injections as in the past.
– take out travel insurance.

Travellers should …
– get advice from a health centre.
– ask their doctor about travel sickness.
– talk with their doctor about any health problems.
– take mild aspirin and cream for insect bites with them.
– put insect repellent on.

– take anti-malarial tablets.
– take antiseptic cream, water purification tablets and toilet paper.
– get health insurance.
– take out travel insurance.
Travellers shouldn't …
– stay out in the sun in warm countries.

10 Visual dictionary

1. check-in counter   2. travel agency   3. suitcase
4. travel plug   5. first aid kit   6. foreign currency
7. antiseptic cream   8. visa   9. passport
10. bandage   11. water purification tablets

19 A LOOK AT LIFE!

3 To have more sleep

to have: more time; more sleep; children; a holiday
to be: in Paris; rich; a sky diver; on holiday
to do: the washing up; the cooking; a lot more
    travelling; more reading; the organising

4 Language summary

She **would** like to be young again.
He'd like to be young again.
We would **like** (**We'd** like) to be young again.
You'd like to be young again.
They'd like to be young again.

He would **not** like to be old.
She **would** not (She **would**n't) like to be old.
You would **not** (You **would**n't) like to be old.
We **would not** (We **wouldn't**) **like** to be old.
They would not (They wouldn't) **like to be old**.

Would she like to be very old? Yes, she **would** / No,
    she **wouldn't**.
Would they like to be very old? Yes, **they would** / No,
    they wouldn't.

5 Would you like to be more intelligent?

	More intelligent? *Yes/No*	*Why?*
Ian	*No*	I'm *very* intelligent.
		I'd go *mad*.
Lyn	*Yes*	I was not one of the
		brightest in the college.
		I *felt* inadequate.
	Man/woman? *Yes/No*	*Why?*
Ian	*Yes*	I'd be *closer* to my 5 children.
Lyn	*No*	I'm *proud* to be a woman.
		I'm happy to stay as *I am*.

7 Paris, of course

1. b   2. a   3. b

9 Visual dictionary

1. to think   2. to relax   3. to travel
4. to read   5. to exercise   6. time for myself
7. a holiday   8. thin   9. tall   10. rich
11. beautiful

20 I'M SO SORRY!

1 I'm ever so sorry!

B
See tapescript for possible answers.

2 It's broken!

Column 2 *What's the matter with it? (short form)*
b. It's got a crack.   c. It's dead.
e. There's a spider in the tin.   h. It's too big.
i. There's a button missing.
j. The ice cream's melted.

Column 3 *What is the matter with it? (long form)*
a. It has stopped.   d. It has broken / It is broken.
f. It has lost one of its legs.
g. It does not work properly.   h. It is too big.

4 At the shops

1. c   2. e   3. b   4. g   5. h   6. d
7. f   8. a

5 Well, do it yourself!

1. lid /ɪ/   2. bed /e/   3. wet /e/   4. fit /ɪ/
5. tin /ɪ/   6. ten /e/   7. pan /æ/   8. pen /e/
9. van /æ/   10. men /e/   11. hat /æ/
12. pet /e/

6 I'm writing to apologise …

A
1. a   2. b   3. c   4. b (*or* c if your teacher
prefers to be informal)

B
Dear Jim,
I'm sorry **I** wasn't able to **at**tend the Engli**sh** classes last
week, but I had **a** very bad cold. I apologise for not
le**tt**ing you **k**now. I hope to be back in class next week.

7 Car-veat emptor!

The two mistakes:
1. three months and one day (not three months and one week)
2. it means 'Buyer be careful' in Latin (not in Italian)
The three pieces of new information:
1. The car was bright red.
2. The car cost $9000.
3. The new engine cost an extra $1000.

8 I bought this car ...

Sample letter:

1 Kings Road
Notre Dame
Montreal
5 July

The Consumer Group
4845 Oxford Avenue,
Montreal

Dear Sir/Madam,

I bought a Cadillac from Apex Autos, Montreal on April 1. Unfortunately, the engine broke down completely on July 1 and experts tell me it is not possible to repair it.

I think it is reasonable to expect a car dealer to tell a buyer all the facts about the condition of a car, but in this case Apex didn't tell me about the engine.

I know that your organisation tries to help people who have problems when they buy things, so I'd like to ask you to write to Apex and ask them to pay for a new engine or exchange the car for a similar one with a good engine.

I hope that you can do something to help me and I'd like to thank you in advance for your help

I look forward to hearing from you.

Yours faithfully,

9 Visual dictionary

1. florist's   2. video rental shop
3. health food shop   4. jeweller's   5. post office
6. newsagent's   7. dry cleaner's   8. antique shop
9. chemist's   10. hairdresser's

21 ALL YOU NEED IS LOVE ... OR MONEY

1 I don't really need it but I want it!

1. need   2. wanted   3. doesn't need
4. would/'d like   5. need   6. need; would/'d like
7. doesn't need; wants   8. wants   9. need
10. want

2 All you need

1. –   2. to   3. –   4. to   5. –   6. to; to
7. to   8. to   9. –

3 Money, money, money

France – franc
Germany – Deutschmark
Brazil – real
Japan – yen
England – pound sterling
Eire – punt
Spain – peseta
Italy – lira
the USA – dollar
Indonesia – rupiah
Russia – rouble
Sweden – kronor
China – yuan

4 We want to get rich ... quickly!

A
to feel
B
to get: rich; worried; better; worse
C
The most common combinations are:
stock exchange; stockbroker
standard of living
long-distance call; long-distance flight
high salary; high price
bank manager; bank account

5 What do you need to be happy?

B

To be happy you need:
nice food   something good to read
someone who loves me   a job that you like
to be healthy   to keep busy   friends
To be happy you don't need:
money   a good job
to be married (wives/husbands)   children

6 My parents wanted me to be a banker

C
1. S   2. S   3. D   4. D   5. D   6. D
7. S

8 Visual dictionary

1. cashier   2. counter   3. coins   4. notes
5. credit card   6. cheque   7. bank statement

22 THE RIGHT CLIMATE?

1 What's it like in Mexico City?

1. c   2. e   3. a   4. b   5. d

2 What's the weather like in your country?

B

1. How many seasons do you have?
2. What is the average temperature in July? (In July what is the average temperature?)
3. What do you do when it is very hot? (When it is very hot what do you do?)
4. What do you do if there is a storm? (If is there a storm what do you do?)
5. Where do you go when there is a national holiday? (When there is a national holiday where do you go?)
6. What's it like in your town in summer? (In summer what's it like in your town?)

3 Snowy weather is good for skiing

A

Some of the possible combinations:
freezing: skiing; walking / a heavy overcoat; gloves; a
    scarf; a pullover
snowy: skiing / gloves; a scarf; a heavy overcoat
cold: walking / gloves; a scarf; a jacket; a pullover
chilly: walking / a pullover; a jacket

cool: tennis; walking; sailing / a pullover; a jacket
warm: tennis; golf; sailing / shorts; a T-shirt
sunny and boiling hot: sailing; sunbathing / a swimsuit;
   a sunhat; shorts
wet: reading / an umbrella

B

1. a sunhat (a swimsuit, shorts are also possible)
2. a heavy overcoat; a scarf; gloves
3. boiling hot
4. wet
5. a pullover; a jacket

4 What do you do when it's hot?

Q1: **What**'s it like in **sum**mer when there are **peo**ple
   on the **bea**ch?
Q2: **What** do you do when it's **hot** and the **sho**ps are
   closed?
Note: The words between the strongly stressed syllables
are spoken quickly to keep the rhythm of the whole
question reasonably regular. Also the most strongly
stressed words often carry the most information.

Reply 1: Erm … it's busy and noisy. I don't like it
      much.
Reply 2: Oh, erm, I go down to the beach and have a
      swim, or I drive up into the mountains.

5 What do you do when you don't know a word?

B

See tapescript for answers.

6 It's the body's largest single organ

A

skin

B

skin: airproof; can repair itself
clothes for skin protection: close-weave fabrics; shirt with a
   collar
products for skin protection: sunblock cream

C

1. F   2. F   3. T   4. T   5. F   6. T
7. F

9 Visual dictionary

1. hurricane   2. wind   3. autumn
4. summer   5. hot   6. earthquake   7. rain
8. cold   9. spring   10. freezing   11. warm
12. winter   13. snow   14. clouds   15. ice
16. flood

23 FESTIVALS

1 Would you like to come to our house?

Inviting: Would you like to come to our house on
   Saturday?
Accepting: Yes, I'd love to. Thanks for asking me.
Declining politely: I'd love to, but I'm afraid I can't.
Reason: I've got to go to work on Saturday.

2 I can't, I'm afraid

See tapescript for answers.

3 Shall I help you with the washing up?

a. 1, 4   b. 6, 5   c. 2, 8   d. 7, 3

4 Word friends

1. birthday party; birthday cake; birthday card
2. Happy New Year; Happy Easter; Happy Birthday;
   Happy Anniversary

5 I have a special thing that I do on my birthday

A

Speaker 1: birthday; a bunch of flowers
Speaker 2: chocolate eggs; Easter
Speaker 3: coffee and cake; Friday nights

B

1. On her own *birthday*, Speaker 1 sends flowers to her
   mother.
2. Speaker 2's parents hide *chocolate eggs* in the *garden* at
   Easter time.
3. Speaker 3 has *three* brothers and they always clear up
   after the family meal on Fridays. Then the sons
   entertain their parents.

6 Festival of tomatoes

C

1. T   2. T   3. F   4. F   5. T   6. T

7 Would you like to come?

B

Example of a reply to the invitation to the party:

Dear Luigi,
Thanks for your invitation to the surprise party for
Mario on July 5th. I'd love to come but I'm afraid I
can't. I'm going to Rome that weekend to see my
mother in hospital. Have a great time. See you soon.
Best wishes,
Claudia

8 Visual dictionary

1. gift   2. card   3. party   4. candle
5. birthday cake   6. Christmas
7. Independence Day   8. dance
9. wedding anniversary   10. bride   11. groom
12. wedding invitation

24 LOOKING AHEAD

1 Past and future

Past	Future
at that time	later this year
then	soon
ago	next year
	five years from now
	in a minute

4 Yes, of course it will, it'll be perfect

See tapescript for answers.

5 I'll learn English or I'm going to learn English

1 am going to / 'm going to
2 will/'ll
3 is going to / 's going to
4 will/'ll

6 Russian electricians

1. I'll (regularly) write long letters (regularly) to lonely Russian electricians.
2. They'll (rapidly) read your long letters (rapidly) and correct the spelling errors.

7 Will people still write letters in ten years' time?

Corrected notes are in *italics*:

Question number: 4
Will children study at home and not at school?
Ian doesn't think so.
Tris says school helps children to learn social skills.

Question number: 2
Will people still use cash?
No, Tris thinks people will use cash less.

Question number: 1
Will people still write letters?
Kate says yes.

Question number: 3
Will city life become more pleasant?
No, Lyn says it will be less pleasant.

8 Will it be one or two?

A

One person: alone; single; individual; divorced (possibly also married)
Two people: couple; pair; married; partners (possibly also divorced)

B

c and d

C

1. c   2. a   3. b

10 Visual dictionary

1. a baby   2. a child   3. a teenager
4. a young married couple
5. a middle-aged woman   6. an elderly couple
7. a very old woman

IRREGULAR VERBS AND PHONETIC SYMBOLS

Irregular verbs

Infinitive	Past simple	Past participle
be	was/were	been
become	became	become
begin	began	begun
bend	bent	bent
bite	bit	bitten
blow	blew	blown
break	broke	broken
bring	brought	brought
build	built	built
buy	bought	bought
can	could	(been able)
catch	caught	caught
choose	chose	chosen
come	came	come
cost	cost	cost
cut	cut	cut
do	did	done
draw	drew	drawn
dream	dreamt	dreamt
drink	drank	drunk
drive	drove	driven
eat	ate	eaten
fall	fell	fallen
feel	felt	felt
fight	fought	fought
find	found	found
fly	flew	flown
forget	forgot	forgotten
get	got	got
give	gave	given
go	went	gone (been)
have	had	had
hear	heard	heard
hit	hit	hit
hold	held	held
hurt	hurt	hurt
keep	kept	kept
know	knew	known
learn	learnt	learnt
leave	left	left
lend	lent	lent
let	let	let
lie	lay	lain
lose	lost	lost
make	made	made
mean	meant	meant
meet	met	met
pay	paid	paid
put	put	put
read /riːd/	read /red/	read /red/
ride	rode	ridden
ring	rang	rung
rise	rose	risen
run	ran	run
say	said	said
see	saw	seen
sell	sold	sold

Infinitive	Past simple	Past participle
send	sent	sent
set	set	set
shake	shook	shaken
shine	shone	shone
shoot	shot	shot
show	showed	shown
shut	shut	shut
sing	sang	sung
sit	sat	sat
sleep	slept	slept
speak	spoke	spoken
spell	spelt	spelt
spend	spent	spent
stand	stood	stood
steal	stole	stolen
swim	swam	swum
take	took	taken
teach	taught	taught
tell	told	told
think	thought	thought
throw	threw	thrown
understand	understood	understood
wake	woke	woken
wear	wore	worn
win	won	won
write	wrote	written

Phonetic symbols

Vowels

Symbol	Example
/iː/	see
/i/	happy
/ɪ/	big
/e/	bed
/æ/	sad
/ʌ/	sun
/ɑː/	car
/ɒ/	pot
/ɔː/	taught
/ʊ/	pull
/uː/	boot
/ɜː/	bird
/ə/	among
	produce
/eɪ/	date
/aɪ/	time
/ɔɪ/	boy
/əʊ/	note
/aʊ/	town
/ɪə/	ear
/eə/	there
/ʊə/	tour

Consonants

Symbol	Example
/b/	back
/d/	dog
/ð/	then
/dʒ/	joke
/f/	far
/g/	go
/h/	hot
/j/	young
/k/	key
/l/	learn
/m/	make
/n/	note
/ŋ/	sing
/p/	pan
/r/	ran
/s/	soon
/ʃ/	fish
/t/	top
/tʃ/	chart –
/θ/	thin
/v/	view
/w/	went
/z/	zone
/ʒ/	pleasure

Stress
Stress is indicated by a small box above the stressed syllable.
Example: advertisement